Worldwide
GUIDE
TO
Homeschooling

2004 A Quick 2005
Reference

Worldwide
GUIDE
— TO —
Homeschooling

**FACTS AND STATS ON THE
BENEFITS OF HOME SCHOOL**

Brian D. Ray, Ph. D.

BROADMAN
&HOLMAN
PUBLISHERS

Nashville, Tennessee

0–8054–2606–X

Published by Broadman & Holman Publishers
Nashville, Tennessee

Dewey Decimal Classification: 649
Subject Heading: HOME SCHOOL

Unless otherwise noted, Scripture quotations are
from the Holy Bible, New International Version,
copyright © 1973, 1978, 1984
by International Bible Society.

1 2 3 4 5 7 8 9 10 08 07 06 05 04

Dedication

Betsy, my best friend and wife, is perfect for me. She loves me through thick and thin. Always expressing confidence and hope in me, Betsy has seen me through a plethora of research, writing, and speaking. She encourages me and makes my work possible. Betsy keeps all our eight children going when I am not with them. And she shows them how to love me and honor me when I am with them. Betsy is and does everything that the right kind of woman should be and do. She thrills me and grounds me, encourages me to go on new advances and stay in tune with the basics, teaches me new things, and listens to me. She is just right for me in every way. Betsy is in a class of her own. Betsy, I love you forever. Brian.

Contents

Preface

Everyone cares about what others think. About what they know. About what they believe. And about what they do. Because it deals with these things, homeschooling has clearly caught the imagination and attention of citizens in many nations.

Whether it is called homeschooling, home education, home schooling, home-based education, or home-centered learning, this age-old practice is experiencing a rebirth around the world. Professionals and skilled workers, those of European, African, and Asian descent, and families who focus on religious belief and those who do not, are all considering the benefits and challenges of homeschooling. They are taking a careful look at the benefits to their children and youth, the benefits to their families, and the benefits to society. They are carefully reevaluating the wisdom and effectiveness of institutional classroom schooling. This book will help them take this look and make this evaluation.

Parents have a deep and abiding interest in their own children's education, in addition to caring about what others think, know, believe, and do. This book will give parents (as well as grandparents and youth) a quick and accurate overview of the homeschool movement and key topics related to it. Parents and youth want to know, of course, how homeschooling will affect a person's academic learning, his or her ability to get along with others, and his or her ability to do well in the adult world. They also want to know how parents and children go about homeschooling and how to get started if they decide to take this route. These questions, and many more, are answered with research and experience throughout this guide.

Policymakers and educators also have a keen interest in the education of children and youth. Related to this, they also want to know whether home-based education will help or hinder their communities and nations. Rather than relying on experiences with only one or two homeschool families, stereotypes, and media reports, policymakers and educators can use the information in this guide to help them gain a broader and richer understanding of the world of homeschooling.

There is one more group: researchers, academics, and curriculum providers studying homeschooling. The number continues to grow, and they need more up-to-date information on this form of education. This book will furnish them with many references, data, and research ideas.

My goal in this book is to provide a reasonable, accurate, honest, and helpful portrayal of home-based education—or homeschooling around the world.

—Brian D. Ray, Ph.D.
January 2004

The Homeschooling Revolution

An increasing number of parents are recognizing the battle that is being waged for their children's hearts and minds—a battle that is played out in their education. While some policymakers and professional educators are calling for institutional schools to exert even more influence in, and control over, the lives of children, others are sounding a clarion call that urges parents to be in charge, knowledgeably and intimately, of their offspring's education.

Parents in droves are taking up the challenge. Home-based, parent-led, family-run education is gaining popularity in many nations, as parents take back control of the way their children are taught from administrators and teachers in both government-run and private institutional schools. Homeschooling allows children and youth to learn in the context of family, home, community, and nation, in a way that respects their individual needs, the proper role of parents in nurturing their children, and the unique contributions a local or extended community makes in the life of a child.

Once commonplace in all nations, homeschooling had waned to near extinction in the mid-1970s. This trend has been dramatically reversed over the past twenty years. Home education is enjoying a surge in popularity and success, which in turn has led to increased interest by the news media. A cover story in *Newsweek* magazine examined home education in October 1998,[1] and *Time* magazine ran a cover story in August 2001.[2] Major newspapers, including the *New York Times*[3] and the *Wall Street Journal*,[4] have run front-page articles on the subject. In a remarkably short time, homeschooling has gone from being obscure and criticized to well-known and praised.

A PROFILE FROM GERMANY

Homeschooling in Germany

Movement toward a homeschool approach to education in Germany began about 20 years ago. Without the support of the law, lawmakers, and attorneys friendly to the cause, however, it failed to grow as it did in America. About 20 years later in 2003, there were about 400 homeschooling families in Germany.

The state strictly controls education. Recently, a German family with 11 children decided to homeschool because of the social agenda being promoted in their school. The state stepped in. Local authorities went so far as to force their way into the home and abduct one of the children and take her to school. Two of the children jumped from the rooftop and fled. Others hid under their beds. Germans and Americans living in Germany asked for help from America's Home School Legal Defense Association, which immediately sent out an alert for American homeschool families to contact the German embassy protesting the harsh action taken by authorities against this family. As a result, the case was dismissed.

The situation in the classroom is becoming increasingly offensive. Public (state) school instruction includes sexual permissiveness, abortion, homosexuality, and bisexuality. Occultist methods are being used by teachers and practiced by students. Drugs and violence abound, and teachers are not able to do anything about it.

Other homeschool cases are pending. Because of the lack of legal representation, a group of Germans and Americans formed Schulunterricht zu Hause (School Instruction at Home), an organization similar to America's Home School Legal Defense Association. This organization is in its infancy and got up and running in 2001.

English Language Contact: Richard and Ingrid Guenther, Schulunterricht zu Hause (School Instruction at Home), Winterhaldenweg 48, 79856 Hinterzarten, Germany; President RA Armin Eckermann; Vice President Chris Klicka; tel. 49–1805–SCHUZH, info@german-homeschool.de, www. german-homeschool.de.

■ ■ ■

Parents who are considering the benefits of homeschooling will find discussion and information in this book to help them make that decision. But there many other categories of individuals will also benefit from this work. Curious journalists and other media persons, policymakers, legislators, professional educators, and doubtful grandparents can use it to understand home-schoolers and the homeschool movement. Marketing strategists can use the information in this book to reach the growing homeschool community. And researchers and homeschool leaders may use each new edition to stay up-to-date on the homeschool movement internationally. Included is an overview of the status of home education in many nations, its history and philosophy, and answers to pressing questions of both parents and young people as they investigate the practical and philosophical issues surrounding home education, particularly in America.

- Why do people homeschool?
- What are current trends in homeschooling, and what is its history?
- How are homeschooled students doing academically?
- What about socialization?
- Are homeschooled students getting into college?
- Am I capable, as a parent, of teaching my own children?
- What about teaching advanced subjects like algebra or chemistry?
- What about special-needs children?
- What about gifted children?
- How do homeschooled children fare in the "real world"?
- What about teenagers who want to home-school?
- Is homeschooling right for us and our family?
- How do we get started homeschooling?

Supplemental information about key support organizations, publications, and services is also provided to help you keep or take back control of the minds, spirits, and bodies of the most precious of all gifts—your children.

A PROFILE

Congressman Jim Ryun and Anne Ryun

United States Congressman Jim Ryun has achieved many unusual things in his life—such as being an Olympic-caliber mile runner. Being an integral part of his children's education by homeschooling them, however, is one of his most treasured experiences. Congressman Ryun and his wife Anne are some of the pioneers of the modern homeschool movement. He recalls, "We were some of the first ones to homeschool in Kansas, so perhaps we encouraged others to take a look at it." It is most certain they did.

The Ryuns have four adult children and two grandchildren. They homeschooled all of their children for at least some of their school years, the youngest from fourth through twelfth grades.

There is more than one reason why they believe in homeschooling. During extensive travel, homeschooling was perfect. While on the road and near the battlegrounds of the Civil War, for example, they could pull out the books they had taken along, read about the battles, walk the sites, and discuss the events and reasons for the war. Another benefit was focusing on the basic three Rs and other academics in the morning, then spending the afternoon exploring special interests—carpentry, baking, sewing, and building a remote-controlled airplane with his boys—as well as doing avid reading.

The Ryuns are confident homeschooling is having a positive impact on society. "Many young adults are very good students as graduates of home education because they have had to develop self-discipline along with self-initiation."

In sum, Congressman Ryun states, "Anne and I simply felt homeschooling was an opportunity for our children to be stimulated academically. It provided them a wholesome spiritual atmosphere, and it kept our family together as a family."

Congressman and Mrs. Ryun treasure the years they had to homeschool their children. It was a response to their God-given responsibility.

You may contact Congressman Jim Ryun in Washington, D.C. at 202–225–6601, or e-mail him at jim.ryun@mail.house.gov.

■ ■ ■

CHAPTER 1

Homeschooling at a Glance

This chapter will provide you with an overview of areas explored in greater depth throughout the book.

How Many People Are Homeschooling Now?

Home-based education is experiencing regeneration and growth at a significant pace in nations as widespread as Australia, Canada, France, Germany, Mexico, South Africa, the United Kingdom, and Japan. Numbers are hard to come by in some nations. An estimated 50,000 to 95,000 students were being homeschooled in Canada during the 2000–2001 conventional school year.[1] In England and Wales, estimates vary widely, from about 13,000 to 50,000.[2] Australian figures are in the range of 35,000 to 55,000. In Germany, a country that remains strongly committed to state education, one organization thinks there are between 500 and 600 homeschooled students.

The United States offers the most accurate information available. During the 2002–2003 school year, the National Home Education Research Institute (NHERI) estimates that between 1.7 and 2.1 million students were being homeschooled in the U.S., in every grade level from kindergarten through twelfth grade.[3] This is a remarkable increase of 500 percent over the number homeschooled in 1990–1991. Indications are that the growth rate is between 7 percent and 15 percent per year.

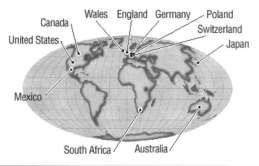

HOME-BASED EDUCATION RENEWING AND GROWING AROUND THE WORLD

What Kind of Families Homeschool?

Families from all social and racial backgrounds are taking on the education of their own children: parents with a grade 10 education, others with Ph.D.s; the wealthy and the less well-off; Christians, humanists, Jews, Mormons, Muslims, and New Age devotees; families with eight children and those with one; married couples and single parents; those in the inner city and those in the wilds of Alaska; sales clerks, public schoolteachers, doctors, and plumbers. Every year the variety broadens and expands.

Are Their Children Getting a Good Education?

Homeschooled students in the U.S. and Canada score 15 to 30 percentile points, on average, above their public school peers. This is true not only in the basics of reading, writing, and mathematics, but also in science, social studies, and study skills. Testing shows that they are also receiving a firm foundation in sound values, in the history of their own nation and the world, and in self-directed learning.

A PROFILE

John Taylor Gatto

John Taylor Gatto was a state (public) schoolteacher in New York City schools for 30 years. Then things changed. His current and historical role in the homeschool movement is as an interpreter of the complex political reality of government schooling as a contradiction of the three traditional purposes of schooling: (1) to make good, moral people, (2) to make good citizens, and (3) to help individuals reach their own personal best.

Gatto is a former New York State Teacher of the Year and three-time New York City Teacher of the Year, and he bases his analysis on extensive personal experience and years of exhaustive research.

At the core of his argument is a massive and deliberate transformation of American schooling, corporation-driven, which took place between 1890 and 1920, to bring about a radical "fourth purpose" in the school equation—to subordinate family and individual goals to the needs of "scientific," corporate, and political managers.

Gatto has a vision of an economy significantly re-localized, a government significantly decentralized and placed largely in the hands of local leadership, and a return to the three traditional purposes of schooling. His latest book is the massive *Underground History of American Education* (much of which applies to education and schooling in many nations), samples of which—and additional information about Gatto—can be obtained free of charge on his Web site: www.johntaylorgatto.com. You may buy his book by calling his toll-free number: 888–211–7164.

■ ■ ■

What About Socialization?

Homeschooled children and youth are involved in an array of activities with children, youth, and adults of all ages. Homeschoolers know that solid social and emotional development is based on interaction with a variety of people and ages in many different settings, not on the stultified peer group setting of typical institutional schools. Home- and family-based activities—including sports, 4-H clubs, Scouts, church activities, gardening, cooperative small-group classes in foreign language and science, and courses at local community colleges—all help to round out the basic home curriculum.

Homeschooled children and youth develop strong ties with their parents and siblings. Research shows that they are also socially, emotionally, and psychologically healthy and strong.

How Well Do Homeschooled Students Fare in College and Adult Life?

In the United States, homeschooled youth are outscoring their public school peers on examinations such as the SAT and ACT, which predict performance in college and university. To date, these tests and research indicate that homeschooled students are performing well in college. In other areas of adult life, they are showing themselves to be hardworking and independent-minded, living off their own earnings, and contributing in positive ways to their families and to society.

What About My Special-Needs Child?

Homeschooling is especially suited to the needs of children who are learning disabled, ADD or ADHD, autistic, inexplicably academically slow, who have chronic illnesses, or who are physically limited or handicapped. Many parents are realizing that individually tailored curricula, flexibility, one-to-one teaching, and the time-efficient nature of homeschooling contribute to making homeschooling an excellent choice for their youngsters who have special needs. Research supports their conviction.

What About My Talented or Gifted Child?

Homeschooling is also growing quickly as the educational practice of choice for parents of children who are particularly gifted or talented. With homeschooling, a student's education can be customized so that he or she can excel at whatever pace is appropriate. The gifted child or youth can quickly become competent in the basics, and then accelerate, through instruction by special tutors or mentors, in any area of special giftedness or interest such as science, history, painting, geography, or instrumental music.

Are Homeschooling Families Helping or Abandoning the Common Good?

Homeschoolers have known all along, and now research and common sense are confirming, that the homeschool movement is having a positive effect on society as a whole. This makes sense. If more and more Johnnys and Lucindas learn to read, write, calculate, and communicate effectively, think critically, be civically involved, get along well with a wide range of age groups, and stand firm on sound values and beliefs, they can only benefit society. The common good is best served when the most children possible are well educated and have sound values that drive their behaviors. Research is suggesting this conclusion about homeschooling.

I Am a Teenager Who Has Been in Public or Private School. How Should I Go About Beginning Homeschooling?

Are you bored at school? Tired of peer pressure? Do you feel you are wasting the best years of your life, with no time for what really interests you? Would you simply like to spend more time with your parents, brothers, and sisters?

There may be many reasons for wanting to get out of institutional schools and into home-based education. This book will give you a good grounding in knowledge about homeschooling, some of the history of institutional schools, and the benefits of home-based education. Remember, it is important that you respect your parents, even if they balk at the idea of your getting out of conventional school ("quitting") and into homeschooling. Help your parents understand your desire by sharing your knowledge and insight into homeschooling.

If you decide to go the homeschooling route, be prepared to be different and to work hard. Be prepared also to experience a new way of life, to feel free, and to be joyful about learning.

What If English Is Not My First Language?

English is not my first language, but I want to homeschool my children. (Or I speak a language different from the dominant one where I now live.)

You are not alone. There are an increasing number of families homeschooling for whom English is their second language. You will become a part of them along with all the others homeschooling in America. (The same applies if you are in another nation and do not speak the main language of where you live.) There are a few steps to consider taking.

First, be of good courage; what you are planning to do is very possible. Second, follow the same basic advice that is set forth in this book. For example, find and participate in a local homeschool support group, read and think about your own philosophy of education, read some magazines and books on homeschooling, and meet and talk with some experienced homeschoolers. Third, you will probably want to arrange things so that you either have an English tutor work on language with your children (and perhaps with you) or plan to have your children involved in some cooperatives with English-speaking children and parents. Fourth, learning with and from you and your children may be the perfect opportunity for which another family, whose first language is English, has been looking; they will be glad to meet you. Finally, remember this principle: you are your child's first and ongoing most important teacher regardless of whether your first language is English (or the language of the nation where you now live). There are many ways to succeed in this situation.

How Do We Start?

Continue reading and thinking about homeschooling and about your own philosophy of education. Second, find a local support group in your town or city, and learn from experienced homeschoolers who are in it. Join a statewide or provincewide homeschooling organization, and attend one of their conferences. Subscribe to a couple of homeschooling magazines. Consider the benefits of joining an organization that focuses on protecting the unalienable and legal rights of parents to direct the education and upbringing of their children. And finally, read the last chapter of this book carefully for detailed information and tips on how to get started.

Wade and Jessica Hulcy

Jessica is a native of Dallas, Texas. She taught for five years in the Dallas public (state) schools in under-privileged areas. There she learned the value of hands-on, discovery-learning methods of teaching. She resigned her teaching post in 1975 when the Lord blessed the Hulcys with their first son, Jason. Wade is a former teacher and coach in the urban schools of Dallas, where he taught for five years before being selected for the principal's program.

They moved from Dallas to Richardson, Texas, to take advantage of the superior school district there for their kindergartener, but they soon came to realize that singing "Here Comes Santa Claus" was not the same as singing "Away in a Manger."

Jessica's friend, Carole Thaxton, was already teaching her son at home so, with much fear and fervent prayer, the Hulcys withdrew their first-grader from public school to try a year of homeschooling. Jessica and Carole wrote their own lesson plans, which they shared with other families. In 1984, they decided to publish their lesson plans as a curriculum. They named their new curriculum KONOS Character Curriculum. Those two little first-graders are now 25 years old and have finished college! The Hulcys have two more boys in college and a 12-year-old at home.

Their teaching philosophy was hands-on, active learning to counterbalance the drudgery of filling out workbooks and textbooks all day long. Their hands-on type of teaching is now termed "Teaching the KONOS Way" by the homeschooling public.

Wade is president of KONOS, a board member of The Texas Homeschool Coalition, and teaches 180 homeschool students physical education each week in three different classes. Listening to mothers on a frequent basis gives him unique insights into the hearts of mothers and the needs of their children. He also has a passion for building families and training fathers to take their God-ordained lead in their families.

You may contact Wade and Jessica at KONOS, P. O. Box 250, Anna, TX 75409, tel. 972–924–2712, wade@konos.com, www.konos.com.

■　■　■

A PROFILE FROM MEXICO

Mike and Pam Richardson

The Richardsons are a family of Christian believers who have chosen to serve the Lord as full-time missionaries in Mexico. Mike and Pam have eight children, five boys and three girls, ages four months to 24 years. In addition to their church planting work, the Richardsons minister to families through homeschooling.

After coming to their field, the Richardsons began to meet a few families from across Mexico who were teaching their children at home. They all had one thing in common. They were struggling because of a lack of Christian education materials and parent resources in Spanish.

Having homeschooled their children since 1986, Mike and Pam felt the Lord was directing them to help these families. In 1996 they began publishing *El Hogar Educador* ("The Home Educator") as a three-page bulletin on homeschooling. It has now grown into a bimonthly magazine and is being sent free of charge throughout Mexico and 19 other countries.

When asked about the diversity in their work, Mike said, "All of our outreach efforts have one thing in common—families. Our desire is to see families come to know our Lord as well as grow in Him—that we might help to win families for Christ and strengthen them by giving them a firm foundation in God's Word."

In addition to live recordings, they also translate, professionally record, and duplicate tapes on homeschooling—a total of 36 messages so far. They organize the only annual national Mexican homeschool conference. In 2000, 911 people attended. Families came from 18 of the 31 states in Mexico as well as a few from the U.S., Spain, and Costa Rica. The Lord has led them not to charge money for the magazine, conference, or the audiocassettes given to each family.

The publication and seminar work continues to grow. *El Hogar Educador* now goes to 28 of the 31 states in Mexico and to 19 other countries. The Lord has given the Richardsons a vision of serving families in every Spanish-speaking country in the world through the resources they produce.

You may contact the Richardsons at Vida Nueva Ministries, 1001 S. 10th St., Suite G-529, McAllen, TX 78501; or Apartado 17, Arteaga Coahuila 25350, Mexico, tel. Mexico 528–483–0377, vnm@character-link.net, www.elhogareducador.org.

■ ■ ■

CHAPTER 2

New Research

Now in the Real world
Adults Who Were Home Educated

For over two decades of the modern homeschool movement, critics and doubters have asked, "But how will they do in the real world?" By this they mean, how will a grown homeschooled child get along in the world of adulthood, after the world of homeschooling that is based in the home and spending much more time with family than do most normal children who attend an institutional school for 13 of their very formative years? A major nationwide study in the United States has recently addressed just this question.

Dr. Brian Ray, in his study entitled *Home Educated and Now Adults: Their Community and Civic Involvement, Views About Homeschooling, and Other Traits,*[1] collected data via a survey on 7,306 adults who had been homeschooled. Of those, 5,254 had been homeschooled for 7 or more years. Of these, he later interviewed 30. The purpose of the study was to describe and gain more understanding about adults throughout the United States who were homeschooled during their elementary and secondary education years. The focus was on their general demographics, attitudes toward their own home-education experience, and success in life.

Methodology

For the main analyses in the report (and for the sake of this chapter in this book), a person was considered to be an adult who was home educated (or home-educated or homeschooled adult) if he or she was at least 16 years old, had finished his or her secondary studies, was homeschooled for at least 7 years during the K through 12 years, was a United States citizen, and submitted a survey (either online or paper) in order to be a part of the study. Complete details on methodology and findings are available in the full-length report, *Home Educated and Now Adults*. Where appropriate and when available, comparable statistics for adults in the United States in general were presented. Comparable statistics are offered in order to provide some meaningful point of reference and not to imply that collection methods or samples used were the same in all respects.

General Demographics and Background of Participants

The average age of the participants was 21; the median number of siblings they had was 3.0; and they were home educated on average for 10.9 years of their K through 12 years. Thirty percent were home-schooled for 7 to 9 years, and 70 percent were home-schooled for 10 to 14 years. The formal educational attainment of these home-educated adults was higher than that of their counterparts in the general American public. In the general U.S. population in the age range of 18 to 24 (the ages which comprised most of the homeschooled in this study), 46.2 percent had attained some college courses or higher; 74.2 percent of the home-educated in this age range had attained some college courses or higher. The most common occupation of these homeschooled adults was full-time student (49 percent of the subjects). The other three most common were homemaker/home educator (7.3 percent), other (7.9 percent), and professional 1 percent (e.g., accountant, RN, artist; 68 percent).

The 10 reasons most frequently cited for why they or their parents decided to homeschool were (a) can give child a better education at home (79.5 percent); (b) religious reasons (76.7 percent); (c) teach child particular values, beliefs, and worldview (73.5 percent); (d) to develop character/morality (69.2 percent); (e) object to what school teaches (61.7 percent); (f) poor learning environment at school (56.1 percent); (g) desire more parent-child contact (56.0 percent); (h) individualize curriculum (48.6 percent); (i) individualize learning environment (46.7 percent); and (j) believe parents should educate children (41.8 percent).

Attitudes Toward Home Education

These home-educated adults had very positive attitudes toward having been homeschooled. Ninety-five percent strongly agreed or agreed with the statement "I am glad I was homeschooled," and 88 percent strongly agreed or agreed with the statement "having been homeschooled is an advantage to me as an adult." Only 5 percent strongly agreed or agreed with the statement "having been homeschooled has limited my educational opportunities," and only 6 percent strongly agreed or agreed with the statement "having been homeschooled has limited my career choices." To the statement "I would homeschool my own children," 82 percent strongly agreed or agreed. Of those who had school-age children, 74 percent had engaged in homeschooling their children; only 9 percent had used only public school for their school-age children.

Interviews with respondents who indicated on their surveys negative attitudes toward homeschooling revealed that they generally were not deeply or adamantly opposed to the practice of homeschooling nor toward having been homeschooled themselves. David Koto (his pseudonym), for example, said in the survey that he was not glad to have been homeschooled. During the interview, his main objection to having been homeschooled was that his parents had strong control over whom he associated with as friends, but then stated that public-school parents may also try to control their child's associations. When asked how homeschooling helped him, David responded: "Definitely academically; I can't deny that at all." After discussing some disadvantages of being homeschooled, David was asked: "Do you think any of these will have a negative effect on you for life?" He responded, "Not really. Probably not."

Style of Living and Civic Involvement

The study found that these home-educated adults were highly involved in community and national life.

For example, 71 percent of subjects were participating in any ongoing community service activity (e.g., coaching a sports team, volunteering at a school, or working with a church or neighborhood association), while only 39 percent of all U.S. adults did so. While 88 percent of these home-educated subjects were a member of any organization (e.g., such as a community group, church or synagogue, union, homeschool group, or professional organization), only 59 percent of all U.S. adults were.

These adults who were homeschooled had a commitment to or tolerance of free expression of viewpoints or beliefs that is about as strong as that of the general public. For example, a higher percent of the homeschooled than the general public (92 percent versus 88 percent) agreed with the idea that "a person should be allowed to make a speech against churches and religion." More of the homeschooled, on the other hand, than the general public (41 percent versus 36 percent) thought that "a book most people disapprove of should be kept out of a public library." Ninety-six percent of the homeschooled thought "a person should be allowed to make a speech against using taxes to feed people or to pay for medical assistance" (and no comparable data were available for the general public).

Several questions were asked about their direct civic involvement. For all civic activities (e.g., working for candidate/political party/political cause, voting in national/state elections) and at all age groups, the home-educated adults in this study were more civically involved than the general national population.

For example, of 18- to 24-year-olds, 13 percent of the home educated while only 1 percent of those nation-wide had worked for a candidate/political party/political cause during the past 12 months; in like vein, 74 percent of the homeschooled but only 29 percent of those nationwide had voted in a national or state election in the U.S. during the past 5 years.

Not only were these home-educated adults more civically involved than the general public, they were more confident than others that they could understand and affect society and government. For example, fewer of the home educated (4 percent) than the general public (35 percent) thought that "politics and government are too complicated to understand." Also, fewer of the homeschooled (6 percent) than the general public (44 percent) agreed with the statement, "My family doesn't have any say in what the federal government does."

Thoughts About Life

Taking all things into consideration, 59 percent of these homeschooled adults, compared to 28 percent of the general population of the same ages, were "very happy" with life. They generally saw life as being more exciting (e.g., exciting, 73 percent of subjects; routine, 26 percent; dull, 1 percent) than did the general population (i.e., 47 percent; 49 percent; 4 percent).

Beliefs and Worldview

Regarding their religious beliefs, a variety of Christian (or Protestant), Roman Catholic, Jewish,

Muslim, and those who said they were "none" or "other" were involved in the study. The majority (93 percent) reported that their parents wanted them to hold basically the same religious beliefs as their parents once they were adults and 94 percent strongly agreed or agreed to the statement, "My religious beliefs are basically the same as those of my parents."

Summary Comments

Since the beginning of the modern homeschool movement, negative critics have claimed that adults who were home educated would shy away from civic involvement, not care about the common good, not be a part of public conversation and debate, and end up being intolerant of allowing others to express their viewpoints. On the issue of whether home-educated adults will be involved in community and civic life, the negative critics may rest at ease based on the findings of this study. Adults who were home educated are avid readers, voters, participants in community organizations, and community servants, and are tolerant of others' publicly expressing various viewpoints. Both those who tend to favor and oppose homeschooling should find this encouraging.

On the issue of whether home-educated adults will come to hold values, beliefs, and worldviews similar to their parents and think well of parent-led, home-based education, the negative critics of homeschooling might continue to be concerned. The participants in this study held worldviews very similar to those of their parents, thought well of having been homeschooled, and largely homeschool their own children.

If a person wants the balance of power over the development of a child's values, beliefs, attitudes, and worldview to be with the state (i.e., government) and those who write its policies, then this study will likely worry him about homeschooling. On the other hand, those who think parents have primary authority over their children's education and upbringing in fundamentals and points of view will perceive this study as suggesting that the homeschooled are successful into their adulthood.

Although some negative critics of homeschooling claim that homeschooling harms the common good and civic involvement of citizens, these critics' actual concern may not be that adults who were home educated will not be civically involved or advance the common good but that those who were home educated *will* be civically engaged and advance values, beliefs, worldview, and social and political practice that is different from the one that the critics of homeschooling had envisioned for the United States (or any other nation).

CHAPTER 3

The History, Growth, and Philosophy of Homeschooling

He asks too many questions. He does not like math. He cannot learn. The teacher says he is "addled"—confused or mixed up. He is the seventh and last child of Samuel and Nancy. They decide to teach him at home; they homeschool the boy—Thomas A. Edison—one of America's most famous inventors.[1] There was a time in the history of today's well-developed nations when parents teaching their own children—instead of sending them away to schools—was common practice. By the late 1970s, however, over 99 percent of school-aged children in the United States, and a similar percentage in other countries, were attending institutional classroom schools. Since then, a great shift in education has taken place, as home and family have again become the center of learning for many. Some would call this change revolutionary. It is the embodiment of the homeschooling movement.

What Is Homeschooling?

Home-based education involves:

- a personal commitment by parents to raise and educate their children,

27

- family-based, and usually parent-led, or sometimes student-led studies,
- a program conducive to individualization,
- a home setting rather than a conventional classroom or institutional setting,
- family participation in neighborhood and community activities, and
- parents, children, and youth using resources that are open to the public to enhance education.

The History and Growth of Homeschooling

People of many cultural heritages, economic means, and religious worldviews are moving quickly to engage their children in home-based education. At current growth rates there may be about 3,000,000 homeschooled students in the United States by the end of the year 2010.

Although homeschooling parents and their children are bucking convention, they are merely recalling the practice and belief of many cultures through the centuries: that parents, families, and closely tied social groups should be the ones to teach each succeeding generation, with the utmost care and dedication, the basic skills of reading and writing, as well as their cultural values, beliefs, and general knowledge.

Parents, teachers, and leaders in every culture recognize that the education, even the indoctrination, of children—the future citizens of their country—

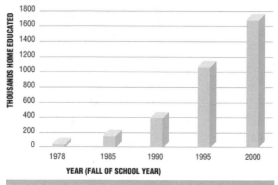

* Number of students homeschooled, grade levels K-12
© 2002 Brian D. Ray. Figure used by permission.

determines which path a nation will follow, whether for good or for evil. Hitler, Lenin, and Mussolini are known for their plans to use schools to advance their own base purposes. Martin Luther wanted to use schools to impress on children the word and mind of God. In America educators such as John Dewey, Horace Mann, and Jane Addams, business leaders, and many other social leaders knew that, if they could design and control the curricula of public schools, they would be able to mold, through indoctrination, the thinking and behavior of the next generation.

John Holt

John Holt (1923–1985) taught in exclusive private schools. Based on his experiences teaching the "best and the brightest," Holt's first book, *How Children Fail*, became a best-seller in 1964 (revised, 1983), launching his career as an education critic and reformer. Unlike other school reformers, Holt believed that segregating children by age, teaching them all the same thing at the same time, and expecting them all to learn equally is "nuts." In *How Children Learn* (1967; revised 1983), Holt noted that children learn best individually or in small groups, not in large bunches, and that the better a teacher can get to know a particular student's interests and abilities, the better a teacher is able to help the student learn. This type of teaching and learning allows the teacher to facilitate and advise while the student learns by doing projects, readings, and working with a variety of people in the real world.

Homeschooling grew out of the alternative school movement of the 1960s and 1970s. Holt supported this movement but moved beyond it. His book *Instead of Education* (1976) outlines and describes the schools and teachers he envisioned. In 1977 he founded one of the nation's first homeschooling periodical, *Growing Without Schooling*, to help bring his vision into reality. Holt is the author of eleven books about children and learning. He wrote, "A life worth living and work worth doing, that is what I want for children (and all people), not just, or not even, something called "a better education."

Many of Holt's writings can be found at Holt Associates/GWS, 2380 Massachusetts Ave., Suite 104, Cambridge, MA 02140, tel. 617–864–3100, toll-free ordering 888–925–9298, www.holtgws.com.

■ ■ ■

Homeschooling: A Rich Cultural Tradition

Many cultures throughout history have practiced home- and family-based education, and some still do. Even during the past few centuries of western civilization, people have practiced forms of education that were clearly parent-controlled or parent-led. Edward and Elaine Gordon make it clear, in *Centuries of Tutoring: A History of Alternative Education in America and Western Europe*, that education centered in and around the home and family has played a key role in society throughout history. The Gordons' brief comments on homeschooling, as practiced at the end of the twentieth century, make it clear that today's home education movement springs from a rich heritage and tradition.[2] It is one more significant expression of the importance of the historical concept and practice of home- and family-based learning through the centuries of western civilization.

Home education, in one form or another, was prevalent in many nations until the late nineteenth century. James Carper points out that, in America, "seventeenth and eighteenth century parents—particularly the father—bore the primary responsibility for teaching their children . . . Christian doctrine, vocational skills, and how to read and, to a lesser extent, write and figure . . . ."[3]

Renowned historian David Tyack explains that during the nineteenth century, "the school was a voluntary and incidental institution: attendance varied enormously from day to day and season to season." Further, the parents and community controlled the school during this period. Schooling or book learning was only a small and often incidental part of a child's total education, for he "acquired his values and skills from his family and from neighbors of all ages and conditions."[4]

"The growth in popularity of compulsory school attendance at the end of the nineteenth and the early twentieth centuries, along with the idea that trained professionals could best teach children, decidedly moved the education of children into the hands of school personnel as the twentieth century began."[5] Home education has always existed in the United States, in spite of the prevalence of school classroom attendance since 1900. Although it is difficult to know how many students were taught primarily at home by their parents during the period from 1875 to 1975, the practice continued to a limited extent. For example, the great distances between homes and schools in the state of Alaska led to the creation, in 1940, of the government-sponsored Centralized Correspondence Study (CCS), which is essentially homeschooling. Those involved in home education across the country today, however, include students far removed from participation in any government-operated program.

Stimuli for the Renewal

A number of factors may account for the sudden growth of home education in the United States during the late

1970s and the 1980s. One study of early published material on home education noted the frequent mention of names such as John Holt, Ivan Illich, and Jonathan Kozol. A direct link was inferred between the public issues of alternative schools, community control, and deschooling that were raised in the 1960s, and the emergence of modern home education: "The early jargon of home education made use of the arguments of the prominent educational reformers"[6] of the 1960s and early 1970s.

Regard for public schools declined during this era of social activism, and concepts such as deschooling and alternative schooling became increasingly prevalent. One researcher has concluded that several people who promoted alternative schools in the 1970s came later to advocate homeschooling.[7]

Since the 1970s, many new homeschool advocates have "found and espoused Biblical and religious rationales . . . . Home schools became grounds of and for ideological, conservative, religious expressions of educational matters, which symbolized the conservative right's push towards self-determinism."[8]

American parents have seen their children slip away from their influence over the past several decades. In order to make sense of the surge in home education, Kirschner surveyed the shifting roles of family and school as educators. He concluded, "We find many Americans turning to 'family values' and scriptural religion in a search for stability and something to believe in. . . . In the home-school movement one finds a hint of optimism in this age of cynicism not seen in quite a while."[9]

Even the secular media came to recognize by the 1990s that they had to address the breakdown of the traditional biblical family that had occurred during the preceding three decades.[10] One sociologist considers home education a way for parents to regain control of their children's and their own lives, a way to make the impact they want on the next generation.[11] This educational life, which integrates parents and children, is, however, contrary to the government-led trend toward the institutionalization and professionalization of education.

This choice is being made by a wide variety of people. For example, it appears that an increasing proportion of blacks, Hispanics, and other minorities are choosing home education. As mentioned in the previous chapter, an indication of the government's level of alarm at the growth in home education is found in the increasing number of tax-funded school-at-home

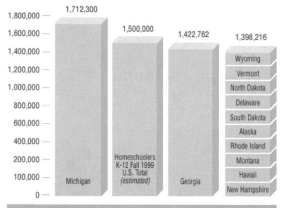

FIGURE 3
NUMBER OF HOMESCHOOL STUDENTS COMPARED TO PUBLIC SCHOOL STUDENTS FROM SELECTED STATES IN THE U.S. FALL 1999

("homeschool") programs being instituted in various American locales to get homeschooling families into state schools.

Public and private educators, the media, policy-makers, politicians, and parents are fascinated with homeschooling. It contradicts what has come to be the norm. Ordinary parents are taking the mystery out of professional teaching, and it seems to be working. In addition, home-based education appears to embody many elements that parents and families have desired throughout the ages, and perhaps especially now, in our highly technological age: a high degree of parental involvement in their children's lives, community-oriented education, success in academics, and an empha-sis on the transmission of cultural values by family, friends, and one's own religious community, rather than by society at large or by a select group of educators.

A PROFILE

Michael P. Farris, J.D.

Mike Farris is one of the best-known names in the international homeschool community. Mr. Farris's prominent and distinguished position in the home-school movement is invigorated by his no-nonsense approach to all sorts of matters. When asked about his vision for parent-led education, he responds: "I got involved in the homeschooling movement in a straight-forward manner. I was an attorney with experience in religious freedom and education litigation. The word got out that I was a homeschooling dad, and people started seeking me out for legal help. They figured that if I was homeschooling, I truly believed in the cause and was not just another lawyer. This is our family's nineteenth year of homeschooling our children. They were right—I truly believe that parents should have the right to educate their own children."

He and his wife Vickie were married in 1971 and have ten children and three grandchildren. They have been homeschooling since 1982.

Mike Farris is president of Patrick Henry College—which opened in September 2000, in Virginia. Farris is also a constitutional lawyer, author of six nonfiction works and three novels, an ordained minister, and a leading pro-family activist on Capitol Hill. He is chairman and general counsel of Home School Legal Defense Association, with a membership of 75,000 families and a staff of 60.

Farris continues in a part-time role as chairman and general counsel of HSLDA after the opening of the college. *Education Week* named Mike one of the most significant 100 "Faces of a Century" in education. He is listed as the person needing prayer on September 18 in the daily prayer guide called *Praying for the World's 365 Most Influential People*. He requests prayer more frequently from all willing persons.

Contact: Patrick Henry College, P. O. Box 1776, Purcellville, VA 20134, tel. 540–338–1776, info@phc.edu, www.phc.edu or the Home School Legal Defense Association, One Patrick Henry Circle, Purcellville, VA 20132, tel. 540–338–5600, mailroom@hslda.org, www.hslda.org.

■ ■ ■

Traits of Homeschoolers and How They Are Changing

A description of any group necessarily involves making generalizations, which provide a level of working knowledge to those on the outside looking in, but often hide significant differences and subtleties among members of that group. When it comes to describing homeschoolers, Bolick's 1987 observation is perhaps even more salient today: "Many homeschoolers are rigidly traditional and scrupulously law-abiding, while others are long-time practitioners of civil disobedience. Some are fervently religious and have removed their children from mainstream schools because they are too secular, while others are nonbelievers who consider the public schools too religious."[12] The following principal characteristics of homeschooling families in the United States emerge as one conducts a synthesis of many studies:[13]

- Both parents are actively involved in home-based education, with the mother/homemaker as the main academic teacher most of the time. Fathers do about 10 percent of the formal teaching of the children.
- Research suggests that 25,000 or more single-parent families were homeschooling in the fall of 1998, and the number is increasing.
- The learning program is flexible and highly individualized, involving both homemade and purchased curriculum materials.
- Some families purchase complete curriculum packages for their children, while others

approach homeschooling with only a small degree of preplanned structure: this is often called "lifestyle of learning" or "unschooling."

- Children are formally schooled three to four hours daily and often spend extra time in individual learning endeavors. The amount of formal or structured learning time is directly related to the student's age.

- The median amount that families spend per child per year for home education, including things such as textbooks, tuition for part-time classes, field trips, and special resources, is about $450, with the large majority spending from $375 to $525 per year, per student.

- As a rule, home-educated students have relatively little interaction with state schools or their services. A minority participate in inter-scholastic activities such as sports and music ensembles in the public (state) schools, or occasionally take an academic course in local schools.

- Children study a wide range of conventional subjects, with an emphasis on reading, writing, math, and science.

- Many students take advantage of the flexibility provided by home education to participate in special studies and events, such as volunteer community work, political internships, travel, missionary excursions, animal husbandry, gardening, and national competitions.

- Children are taught at home for at least four to five years. Most parents intend to home educate their youths through the high school or secondary years.

- On average, there are 3.0 to 3.3 children in the family.
- Male and female students are equally represented.
- At least 95 percent of homeschooling families are headed by a married couple.
- Formal instruction typically begins at five to six years of age. The individualized nature of homeschooling allows parents to begin formal instruction when their child is ready, rather than at a state-specified age, and to proceed at a pace most suitable for the child.
- About 70 of students are between the ages of seven and 13. Research suggests that the age distribution is beginning to approximate that of the general population.
- The typical homeschooling parent has attended or graduated from college. About half of home educators have earned a bachelor's or higher degree. However, there are significant numbers who have only a high school education.
- The total annual household income is under $25,000 for about 18 percent of the families; $25,000 to $49,000 for about 44 percent; $50,000 to $74,000 for about 25 percent, and $75,000 or more for about 13 percent. This is close to the median (typical) income for American families.
- Over 75 percent regularly attend religious services. The large majority are of the Christian

faith and place a strong emphasis on orthodox and conservative biblical doctrine. Significant and increasing numbers of agnostics, atheists, Buddhists, Jews, Mormons, Muslims, and New Agers also homeschool their children.

• In terms of racial/ethnic background, it appears that currently over 90 percent are white/non-Hispanic. A rapidly increasing number of minorities, however, are engaging in home-based education.

In summary, a wide variety of individuals are involved in homeschooling in the U.S., just as the U.S. is comprised of a multiethnic, multiracial, pluralistic population. Nothing in the research literature suggests that homeschooling families are, as a group, outlandish with respect to the characteristics previously summarized. They are part of mainstream America, except for their attitude towards the education and nurturing of their children.

Why Do Families Choose to Homeschool?

John Taylor Gatto is a renowned educator and three-time public (state) school teacher of the year for both New York State and New York City. After he had spoken in Nashville, a mother named Debbie gave him the following handwritten note:

We started to see Brandon flounder in the first grade—hives, depression. He died every night after he asked his father, "Is tomorrow school too?" In second grade the physical stress became apparent. The teacher pronounced his problem Attention Deficit Syndrome. My happy, bouncy child was now looked at as a medical problem, by us as well as the school.

A doctor, a psychiatrist, and a school authority all determined he did have this affliction. Medication was stressed along with behavior modification. If it was suspected that Brandon had not been medicated he was sent home. My square peg needed a bit of whittling to fit their round hole, it seemed.

I cried as I watched my parenting choices stripped away. My ignorance of options allowed Brandon to be medicated through second grade. The tears and hives continued another full year until I couldn't stand it. I began to homeschool Brandon. It was his salvation. No

FIGURE 4
REASONS PARENTS AND YOUTH CHOOSE TO HOMESCHOOL

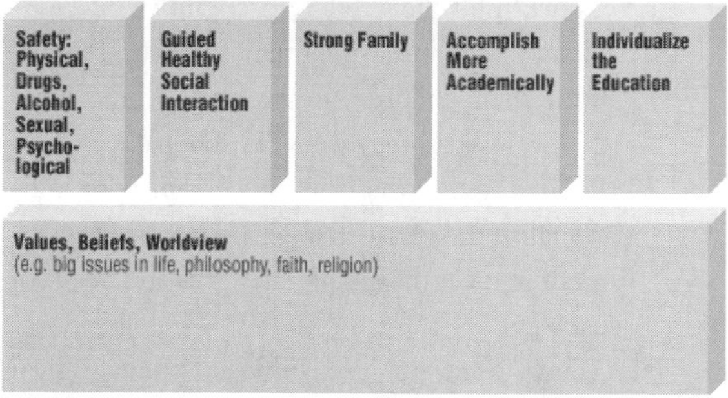

Safety: Physical, Drugs, Alcohol, Sexual, Psychological	Guided Healthy Social Interaction	Strong Family	Accomplish More Academically	Individualize the Education

Values, Beliefs, Worldview
(e.g. big issues in life, philosophy, faith, religion)

© 2002 Brian D. Ray. Figure used by permission.

more pills, tears, or hives. He is thriving. He never cries now and does his work eagerly.[14]

Not many schoolteachers, administrators, or parents want to talk about things such as this. However, many who are now adults experienced that dying feeling themselves as children. They know it is part of why they hated school or still feel queasy when they think back to their school days. The happy memories of school days are, for great numbers of adults, a myth.

As we have seen, the stereotypes regarding who is involved in homeschooling are breaking down. Multiple studies make clear the main reasons parents choose to homeschool (Figure 4):[15]

- The most frequently cited reason is concern for the development of their children's values and way of life. They desire to teach and transmit their philosophical, religious, or cultural values, traditions, and beliefs, and a particular worldview, in a preferred moral environment.
- Concern for their children's cognitive development is the next important reason. Parents want their children to accomplish more academically than they would in schools.
- Related to this, they want to customize or individualize the curriculum and learning environment to meet the unique strengths and needs of each child.
- Many want to use different pedagogical approaches.

- They want to enhance family relationships between children and parents and among siblings, through more time spent together.
- They want to provide guided and reasoned social interactions with youthful peers and adults, thus avoiding unnecessary and perhaps harmful peer pressure that may occur in an institutional setting.
- An increasing number of parents are concerned about the safety of their children, because of physical violence, drugs and alcohol, psychological abuse, and improper sexuality.

Research also shows that many parents' and youths' reasons for homeschooling change or mature over time.

A FIRST-PERSON PROFILE

Samuel Blumenfeld

Back in the 1970s, I became aware of America's reading problem and decided to help parents teach their children to read properly with intensive phonics at home. As a result, thousands of homeschooling parents have used my books and succeeded in raising literate children.

I also became aware that the reading problem resulted from the schools' faulty teaching methods. The problem has persisted because our government system is controlled by leftists, dedicated to dumbing down the nation so that we can be led without resistance into a socialist system of government.

I now believe that we must strive for educational freedom, for a government education system is basically incompatible with the principles and values of a free society. The aim of my work as a writer and activist is to make sure that future American children inherit a free society and not a socialist tyranny.

In addition, children in the state schools are at risk in four serious ways:

- Academically, because of faulty teaching methods that produce reading disability, ineffective math skills, and a socialist view of history.
- Spiritually, because the schools are doing everything in their power to undermine the Christian beliefs of the children through evolution, humanism, eastern religion, magic circles, et cetera.
- Morally, because of easy access to drugs in schools and explicit sex education that encourages premarital sex experimentation.
- Physically, because of the violence in the schools, where Christian children have been targeted by satanists for harm and even murder.

I am the author of eight books on education, including: *Is Public Education Necessary? NEA: Trojan Horse in American Education; The Whole Language/OBE Fraud; Homeschooling: A Parents Guide to Teaching Children; How to Tutor;* and *Alpha-Phonics: A Primer for Beginning Readers.*

Besides being a writer, I served in the U.S. Army in World War II and took part in combat during the last weeks of the Italian campaign. I invite you to visit my Web site (www.howtotutor.com). I also write a weekly column for *World Net Daily* (www.worldnetdaily.com), a conservative Internet newspaper. To gain access to my articles, click on "commentaries," then click on my name in the left margin. That will take you to my archive.

■ ■ ■

A PROFILE

Gregg Harris

"The noble man makes noble plans and by noble deeds he stands" (Isa. 32:8). Gregg Harris was a young pastor in Dayton, Ohio, when he and his wife Sono first began homeschooling. That was in 1980. After a frustrating experience with "church preschool socialization," they enrolled their first son, Joshua, who at the time was just six years old, as the first and only student in Dayton Christian Schools Home School Extension Program (DCS), working closely with the school superintendent, Bud Schindler. Homeschooling was illegal. But in the light of God's Word, it was also the right thing to do.

The following year, Gregg was asked by DCS to present an introductory workshop on homeschooling for 17 new families who wanted to join the Home Schooling Extension Program. Twenty-nine people attended that first Home Schooling Workshop. From this small beginning, over 250,000 parents would receive a distinctively Christian orientation on why and how to teach their children at home. Gregg's Friday evening presentations, "Why Home School Your Child?" and "The Battle for Your Child," which opened up the stories of Noah and Lot, turned many thousands of passive fathers into actively involved homeschool dads.

In 1983 Gregg resigned from his pastorate to devote his full time to promoting homeschooling. In the fall he moved his family to Gresham, Oregon, to work more closely with other national homeschool leaders who at the time lived in the Pacific Northwest. Working initially with small, local home-school support groups, Gregg traveled nationally to use his early events as a catalyst to help establish Christian Home School Associations in 35 states. He also worked with Bud Schindler and Doug Horney at the 1983 Association of Christian Schools International Leadership Conference to draft the historic resolution to allow ACSI Schools to support homeschoolers "if they wanted to." He then encouraged homeschoolers nationally to unite with and support their local Christian schools wherever practical. His workshops and their exhibit halls helped many curriculum publishers, some of whom were initially unwilling to knowingly sell materials to home-schoolers, meet and better understand homeschool parents.

At the same time, Gregg's workshops helped *The Teaching Home* magazine, Home School Legal Defense Association (HSLDA), *Practical Home-schooling* magazine, and later the National Home Education Research Institute (NHERI) to reach the growing Christian homeschooling movement. His columns and articles on homeschooling appeared in many magazines, and he was a guest on many national radio programs. In 1987 Gregg wrote *The Christian Home School*.

As the homeschooling movement matured, the need for a homeschool publisher for books and materials other than curriculum became obvious. Gregg then launched Noble Publishing Associates under which many classic homeschool titles were introduced, such as *The Right Choice: Home Schooling* by Christopher Klicka, *Fun Physical Fitness* by Sono Harris, and *The Original 21 Rules of This House* written by Gregg and illustrated by his son Joshua at age 14.

Beginning in 1995, the need for an annual introduction to homeschooling had waned. The state homeschool organizations, curriculum fairs, and regular support group meetings were well established. Gregg had worked himself out of a job.

In 1998 he founded Noble Institute for Leadership Development, a nonprofit educational foundation devoted to restoring the family to its proper place of influence in the local church. Also in 1998, under the auspices of Noble Institute, Gregg joined with other families to plant Household of Faith Community Church, an age-integrated church in Gresham, Oregon, where he now serves as a teaching elder. Gregg can be contacted for seminars and speaking engagements at: Noble Institute, 6920 S.E. Hogan Road, Gresham, OR 97080, or by e-mail at ghatclw@aol.com.

■ ■ ■

CHAPTER 4

Benefits to Children and Youth

Are They Learning Without Licensed Teachers?

Does homeschooling work, academically? Many school teachers, administrators, and parents wonder whether ordinary mothers and fathers, who are not government-certified teachers, are capable of teaching their children after age six. Is it possible for adults without specialized, college-level training in teaching to help their children learn what they need to learn?

Media reports, covering events such as citywide, even national, spelling and geography bees, have distorted the image of homeschooled youngsters by making some of them look like champions and stars. In reality, their academic success is not always so outstanding. Nonetheless, it is worthy of note.

Dozens of studies have now been completed, often involving analyses of standardized achievement test scores. On average, homeschooled students outscore their public (state) school peers by 15 to 30 percentile points (Figure 5).

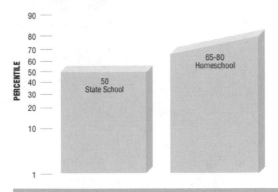

A FIRST-PERSON PROFILE

Eric and Joyce Burges Family

Nearly 12 years ago when Eric Jr.'s guidance counselor called us to meet her at the school, I knew something was up! I, his mother, went reluctantly but determined at that very moment that I had had enough of this repetitious educational merry-go-round. Nonetheless, I went with an open mind.

While Eric Jr. was in his middle school years (our other children were in elementary school—I was repeating the same actions at their school as well), I was at the school nearly every day—helping teachers, working in the office, being the PTO president

(Parent Teacher Organization), and so forth. All of this was to help my son and also to let the teachers see that I was a parent who was a doer. However, none of this came out to a positive end for our family. I began to notice that the teachers did not want me around; they revealed this subtly, yet defiantly. Having me around was putting pressure on them to teach my son and not to fool around—because they knew that I knew what the real deal was. And this was it: I was there to make sure my son was giving his all and that each teacher was doing his or her job.

Now, when he entered the first semester of high school, the "big" teachers let us know at first sight and in so many words that "they appreciated our love and concern for our son—but that we should leave the education of our son to them." Soooo, we swooned and left the educational process to them, with the exception of normal checking and showing up every now and then. But very soon we were to become quite desperate, a desperation that would lead to our destiny—homeschooling.

When we met the guidance counselor, she informed us that Eric Jr. was not at the 3.0 GPA that he needed to stay in such a "magnet, gifted and talented, private-donors school." She recommended two choices—retain Eric Jr. in the ninth grade or send him to a school "way across town." My response to her was, "Excuse me, Ma'am, but neither of these choices is what I will do for my son; thank you for your time." That evening when we arrived home, I immediately asked Eric if I could homeschool our son. And the rest is history.

I want every person on the face of this earth to know that homeschooling is a viable choice for educating children. When I needed this choice, it was there for me. Some parents think that homeschooling is against the law. They do not know that homeschooling is their right. This is my goal. I do not get weary in doing this great work. When the enemy wanted Nehemiah to come to them, he asked them, "Should I stop this great work that I am doing to come and see you." This is my response to people: Many times I am asked, "Why do I continue to homeschool when so many that started with you have chosen to place their children back in school?" I am a mother—the education of my children is my responsibility. I take great pleasure in knowing that I can contribute just a little to the kingdom of God by investing in His greatest treasures—my children, His children. And I do not stop there. Any child that I can help teach to read, to understand history, to realize that science is observing the things around you, encouraging a child to think logically and reasonably—I can think of no greater joy than to lead a child into learning the good things in this life. This is my lift, my joy! Yes, I was thrust onto this path and for this reason. God deserves all of the glory.

Eric and Joyce Burges are black Americans residing in Baton Rouge, Louisiana. Eric is employed by the Department of Transportation in Louisiana, and Joyce is a stay-at-home homemaker of 17-plus years. Both are musicians, and Eric is a licensed minister. They are the parents of five children ages 25 through 6 years of age, and they began homeschooling in 1991. They eventually served as president of the Christian Home

Educators Fellowship of Louisiana, and they recently founded the National Black Home Educators Resource Association (NBHERA) described elsewhere in this book).

■ ■ ■

The following study results indicate that the answer to our opening question is a resounding yes (Figure 6). Parents are succeeding in teaching their children and in teaching them well.

The Stanford Achievement Test scores of hundreds of home-educated students, grades K-12, in Washington State over several years show that they consistently score above the national average in reading, language, math, and science, with the median score at about the 67th percentile on national norms.[1] The national average for public school students is about the 50th percentile.

Home-educated students across Canada performed well above average in all academic subject areas.[2] For example, they scored, on average, at the 89th percentile in reading, the 79th in math, the 82nd in science, and the 81st in social studies.

A California study found no significant differences in the intelligence and achievement test scores between homeschooled nine-year-olds and their private-school peers.[3]

Students in Alaska's Centralized Correspondence Study have consistently scored significantly higher than conventional-school students in Alaska and nationwide on the California Achievement Test in math, reading, language, and science.[4]

State departments of education, such as those in Oregon and Tennessee, often report that the home-educated students for whom they have records score well above average on standardized achievement tests.[5]

The most in-depth nationwide study to date examined the achievement of home-educated students on standardized academic achievement tests. Data were collected on 1,657 families, involving 5,402 children. These students scored, on the average, at these high percentiles:

- total reading, 87th
- total language, 80th
- total math, 82nd
- total listening, 85th
- science, 84th
- social studies, 85th
- study skills, 81st
- basic battery (reading, language, and mathematics combined), 85th
- complete battery (all subject areas in which student was tested), 87th.[6]

Notably, the home-educated did quite well in subjects that skeptics often consider to be too difficult for the untrained to teach, such as mathematics and science, and in areas that skeptics think home educators are not interested in teaching, such as cross-cultural studies and social studies.

The Home School Legal Defense Association (HSLDA) reported in 1994 on the Iowa Test of Basic Skills (ITBS) scores, for several subjects, obtained by

16,311 home-educated students in grades K through 12. The basic battery scores, by grade level, ranged from a low of the 62nd percentile to a high of the 87th percentile, with the majority of percentile scores in the 70s. These lower scores, as compared with the author's study in the previous point, may be explained by the fact that the author's studies involved voluntary participation, which tended to include students whose achievement scores were slightly higher than those in the general home-education population that this HSLDA report might have represented.[7]

A more recent study of the ITBS scores of about 21,000 home-educated students nationwide found the students' average percentiles were in the mid-60s to mid-70s. At each grade level, the percentile corresponding to the median scaled score was typically in the 70th to 80th percentile range.[8]

In other studies home-educated students have recorded these achievements in standardized tests:

- Indiana: averaged at the 86th percentile on the basic battery[9]
- Massachusetts: averaged at the 85th percentile on the basic battery[10]
- Montana: at the 72nd and 70th percentile on the basic battery[11]
- North Dakota: averaged at the 85th percentile[12]
- Oklahoma: averaged at the 88th percentile in the combination of their reading, language, and mathematics performance[13]
- Pennsylvania: at the 73rd to 86th percentiles[14]

FIGURE 6
SEVERAL STUDIES OF HOMESCHOOL & PUBLIC SCHOOL TEST SCORES (ACADEMIC ACHIEVEMENT, GRADES K-12, AVERAGE)

Study	Percentile
Alaska *Alaska Department of Education '93*	78
Canada *Ray '01*	79
Florida *Ray '94*	72
Indiana *Ray '97*	86
Maine *Ray '94*	71
Massachusetts *Ray '98*	85
Montana *Ray '95*	70
Oregon *Oregon Department of Education '98*	75
Tennessee *Tennessee Department of Education '98*	73
U.S. *Ray '94*	77
U.S. *Ray '97*	84
U.S. *Rudner '99*	75
Virginia *Ray '94*	89
Washington *Wartes '91*	67
Washington *Washington State Superintendent of Public Instruction '85*	58
Public School Students	50

PERCENTILE: 1 10 20 30 40 50 60 70 80 90

* Used Basic Battery scores if available (or general average of the three R's)
© 2002 Brian D. Ray. Figure used by permission.

Data suggest that the home-educated are also doing well academically in the United Kingdom.[15]

While not all studies show home-educated students scoring above average, overall research clearly indicates that homeschooled students perform at least as well as, and usually better than, their conventionally schooled counterparts, in the subject areas considered to be the basics of American education, and the essential tools for success in college and in American society.

What About Socialization?

It is well-known among educators, and many others, that there is a hidden curriculum in the schools, having more to do with values and acculturation than with reading, writing, and arithmetic. It has to do with how people behave and with what understanding of reality and society guides their thinking. The hidden curriculum affects the psychological and spiritual development of a child. While some have tried to argue that the public school environment and curriculum are value-neutral and religion-neutral, most scholars and educators have come to recognize this is not true. Warren Nord, of the department of philosophy of the University of North Carolina, stated: "Indeed, I will argue that at least in its textbooks and formal curriculum students are *indoctrinated* into the modern (secular) worldview and against religion."[16] All of this is part and parcel of socialization.

When someone asks of home education, "What about socialization?" he or she usually means, "How will these children learn to get along with others when they are not in large, age-segregated groups of their peers most of the day?" He might mean, "How will this home-educated child learn to accept the American—or Canadian, German, or Japanese—way of thinking and living?" Of course, the questioner has already made some unspoken assumptions:

- that a conventional school classroom is the best setting for learning how to get along with others;
- that a child in such a classroom will learn best how to stand on his own;
- that an age-segregated situation with a government-certified teacher is best for learning how to function and think in society; and
- that the conventional classroom setting is the healthiest setting for the psychological development of a child who is trying to become a mature adult in a democratic republic.

"What about socialization?" is a perennial question asked of home educators and their children. Several researchers have explored the self-perceptions, which are related to socialization, of the homeschooled. Their findings should help put this question to rest.

Regarding the significant aspect of self-concept in the psychological development of children, several studies have revealed that the self-concept of home-schooled students is significantly higher than that of public school students. One researcher concluded: "A low anxiety level could be a contributing factor. . . .

More contact with significant others, parental love, support, and involvement, peer independence, and a sense of responsibility and self-worth may be other contributing factors."[17]

Their academic self-concept, at the 72nd percentile, was above the national average and was positively related to achievement.[18] They have above average self-esteem, in multiple studies.[19]

They are "not isolated but active, contributing members of society, even in childhood. Ninety-eight percent are involved in weekly church meetings and other activities that require interfacing with various ages and settings."[20]

Private school nine-year-olds were seen to be more influenced by or concerned with peers than a comparative home-educated group. It appears that home-educated children perceived their parents as primary authority figures more often than did the private school children.[21]

Homeschoolers' self-concept was just as strong as that of private school students and higher than that of public school students, all of whom in this study attended Baptist (Christian) churches. All of the three groups were above national norms.[22]

An evaluation of the communication skills, socialization, and daily living skills of demographically matched publicly schooled and home-educated students revealed that "the home-educated children in this sample were significantly better socialized and more mature than those in public school. The immediate implication is that homeschool families are providing adequately for socialization needs." Further, the researcher stated more strongly, "The findings of this study indicate that children kept home are more mature and better socialized than those who are sent to school."[23]

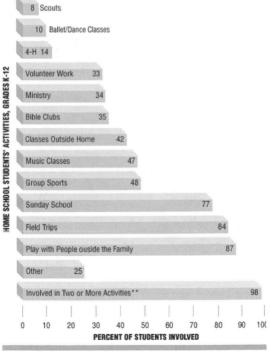

FIGURE 7
HOMESCHOOLERS' ACTIVITIES AND COMMUNITY INVOLVEMENT

HOME SCHOOL STUDENTS' ACTIVITIES, GRADES K-12

Activity	Percent
Scouts	8
Ballet/Dance Classes	10
4-H	14
Volunteer Work	33
Ministry	34
Bible Clubs	35
Classes Outside Home	42
Music Classes	47
Group Sports	48
Sunday School	77
Field Trips	84
Play with People ouside the Family	87
Other	25
Involved in Two or More Activities**	98

PERCENT OF STUDENTS INVOLVED

*Based on Ray, 1997

Institutionally schooled students have been shown to receive significantly higher problem-behavior scores than their home-educated age mates. The conventionally schooled tended to be considerably more aggressive, louder, and more competitive than were the home-educated. Larry Shyers, the author of this study, noted that his findings draw into question the assumption made by many people that traditionally educated children have better social adjustment than those who are home-educated.[24]

In summary, as far as researchers have found, the home-educated are doing well in their social, psychological, and emotional development. Perhaps the fact that most of these children have siblings and are engaged in a variety of social and community activities makes the research findings on socialization not surprising (Figure 7).[25]

There have been very few negative findings in this area. A small study of six- to 10-year-olds (56 home-schooled and 44 conventionally schooled children) in Michigan revealed that the home-educated were lower in some of the self-perception domains tested when compared to the conventionally schooled group. The authors pointed out that their findings regarding perceived competence seemed to contradict findings by a number of other researchers.[26]

In a study of families drawn from the directory of one nationally circulated homeschooling magazine, one-fifth of the parents said there was some form of social isolation involved.

However, many of these parents explained that the problem was not isolation itself but the challenge of the effort parents needed to expend, in order to provide an acceptable type and degree of social contact. It is significant, too, that the parents did not say that this isolation resulted in children with poor social skills.[27]

Can Children with Special Needs Do Well in Homeschooling?

To date there is little research into the homeschooling of children with special needs or those who are talented or gifted. What there is, though, speaks well of the effects of this type of education.

A mother recently wrote to me: "Can I successfully homeschool my Asperger Syndrome/ADHD child? He is nine years old and is number three of four children. Currently he is in a public [state] mainstream school with two hours support every day. Among other situations he has been hit by a relief teacher and yelled at by two experienced teachers and forced eye contact. He is definitely not a behavior problem at school and is very well mannered and polite. He is just autistic with slow processing time and cannot verbalize his feelings or needs."

This kind of story abounds. It is not necessarily the case that school educators are bad persons or would be particularly incapable of helping such special children if they only had one or two at a time to help. This, however, is not the case in institutional schools and never will be—one reason why homeschooling is fast gaining popularity with parents of children with special needs.

Some work has been done on elementary and junior high students with mental or physical delays,

Attention-Deficit/Hyperactivity Disorder (ADHD), or disabilities, in both homeschooling situations and public school special-education programs. The purpose of such studies is to determine whether parents, who were not certified as professional educators, provided students with instructional environments that facilitated the acquisition of basic skills. Their findings are encouraging for all homeschooling parents but especially for those with special-needs children:

- Homeschooled students were involved in academic engaged time (AET) 59 percent of the time versus 22 percent of the time for public school students. The "home school students made more [academic achievement] gains in comparisons involving reading, the one involving math, and three of four in written language. The remaining written language comparison . . . involved equivalent home school and public school gains."[28]
- "Generally, the measures of classroom ecology and achievement showed that home schools, when compared to special education programs, provided equal if not more advantageous instructional environments for children with learning disabilities."[29]

It was concluded that parents could create powerful instructional environments for their children at home.

While researchers use conservative terms to state the success that parents have in homeschooling their learning-disabled children, a rapidly increasing number of families with special-needs children are eagerly choosing this option.

A PROFILE

Tom and Sherry Bushnell Family

You can do it! Special-needs children can be home-schooled. Children with challenges need tender care in character development and academics, as they are able.

Tom and Sherry Bushnell are directors of the National Challenged Homeschoolers Associated Network, NATHHAN. The Lord has blessed them with nine children, 3 of whom are adopted and have special needs. The children range in age from 17 to three. All are taught at home. Therapies are done at home without the help of public programs. The Bushnells are blessed with the opportunity to encourage other parents with special-needs children to put together a private education program, learning at home.

Tom Bushnell shares, "It is our prayer that Christian families with unique children realize that they can home educate. The resources to do this are abundant. Homeschooling can offer Christian character development while programs in many other educational settings cannot. Wisely using the early years can make a big difference whether or not our challenged children will be a blessing at home when they are grown."

As you can see, the folks at NATHHAN are specially motivated by the truths of the Bible—at the same time, they are open to and enjoy helping parents and children of any religious faith. NATHHAN is an organization of 12,000 families with special-needs children, supporting one another. A quarterly magazine, lending library, and NATHHAN family directory is available for a membership fee of $25.00 a year. Contact: NATHHAN, P. O. Box 39, Porthill, ID 83853, tel. 208–267–6246, www.NATHHAN.com.

■ ■ ■

Homeschooling the Talented and Gifted

Another group of students, the talented and gifted (TAG), also appear to be a part of the swelling ranks of the home-based education community. In 1984 Katheryn Kearney, now an instructor at Iowa State University, wrote, "No less a gifted inventor than Thomas Edison was taught at home by his mother, after she removed him from school when his teacher said he was 'addled.'" Kearney interviewed two families with gifted children to explore what they did and to discover what contributed to their success. She says: "Both families designed an extensive, individualized curriculum for their children, taking into account special abilities and interests."[30]

Jacque Ensign studied both special-needs and gifted students who were home-educated and concluded that the hallmarks of the educational philosophies and pedagogies of the homeschoolers in this study are:

- a focus on the whole child rather than primarily on the child's disability or extreme ability;

- individualized attention; and
- care, patience, and respect for the child, allowing the child to lead the teacher in both the timing and the content of what he or she is ready to be taught.[31]

"The educational outcomes for these homeschooled special education students are self-confident students who have developed academic skills at very uneven rates but who have usually achieved academic excellence by the end of high school."[32]

In addition to this limited research on TAG students, numerous writers in the field have listed the names of famous gifted people who were homeschooled and have suggested that homeschooling is a good option for many gifted children.[33]

A PROFILE

"Little Bear" (Richard Wheeler)

Richard "Little Bear" Wheeler is one of the most popular homeschool and family conference speakers in the United States, and people in other nations are quickly catching onto his vision for education. In his autobiography, *The Little Bear Story: The Adventures of a Retarded Gopher Skinner*, he gives testimony like this:

My early school years were like being in the military. From what I've been told, I was definitely a handful, even for those Sisters who were trained to combat and deal with problem children. They had to bring out their entire arsenal of dastardly tools to shape, mold, and break the wild stallion in my undisciplined nature. We didn't have fancy medical terms that labeled dysfunctional children in those days (the 1950s). I am convinced that it was because of my behavior that medical science invented terms like hyperactive, attention deficit disorder, and dyslexia, as well as the drug Ritalin to sedate children. I still have my elementary Catholic school report cards with horrible grades and notes written on the back informing my mother that I was "retarded." This caused my mother to take me to the family doctor so he could tell her what to do with her "retarded" son.

The doctor psychoanalyzed me and declared to my mother that I was a "normal" child. He further related his suspicion that perhaps she was the one with brain damage since she had brought me to see him for my "retardation." Needless to say, we were both relieved to find out that we were sane. Note that we were "sane" but not necessarily "normal" individuals.

Today the Children's Social Services Division would have had those teachers arrested for the things they put me through. What I considered to be my best behavior was most intolerable to the teachers. After my punishment, I was sent back to my desk to hang my head in shame and wonder what was wrong with me. In my mind, as well as my mother's and the doctor's, I was perfectly normal. I guess I was just too "retarded" to consider that something was wrong with me.

Richard "Little Bear" Wheeler is a skilled storyteller who keeps audiences of all ages enthralled and amazed by his costumes, props, and rapid-pace, nonstop, and entertaining language. This evangelist/historian has integrated his theological and theatrical training to reach believers with a message that will alert, equip, and commission them in their God-ordained responsibility to raise a generation that will uphold the standards of Christ Jesus. Richard Wheeler married Marilyn, and they have three children, all of whom they have homeschooled. They live in Bulverde, Texas, just north of San Antonio. He may be contacted at Mantle Ministries, 228 Still Ridge, Bulverde, TX 78163, tel. 830–438–3777, www.mantleministries.com.

■ ■ ■

How Will the Home-Educated Fare in the Real World and College?

Linda Montgomery, principal of a private high school, was one of the first to look to the future and adulthood of the home-educated. She did this by investigating the extent to which homeschooled students were experiencing conditions that foster leadership in children and adolescents who attend institutional schools. Her findings on 10- to 21-year-olds suggested that the home-educated are certainly not isolated from social and group activities with other youth and adults. They were quite involved in church youth group and other church activities, jobs, sports, summer camps, music lessons, and recitals. She concluded that it appears homeschooling nurtures leadership at least as well as does the conventional system.[34]

Susannah Sheffer's book on her study of home-schooled adolescent girls is replete with these girls' own words and interpretive comments by the researcher. Sheffer begins her report by citing the work of Carol Gilligan and her colleagues in the Harvard Project on Women's Psychology and Girls' Development who, lamenting, "have written about girls' 'loss of voice' and increasing distrust of their own perceptions." Sheffer suggests that the great difference in structure and function—the way things work, the relationships people have, expected behaviors, and the roles people play—between homeschooling and conventional schooling may explain why she found so many of these home-educated adolescents to have not lost their personal voice and personal sense of identity.

Meredith is a 14-year-old quoted in Sheffer's book: "I was worried that I would become a typical teenager if I went to school" and "I think some people would have seen [school] as my opportunity to 'be like everybody else.' But I didn't want to be like everybody else." Sheffer concludes, "Throughout this book the home-schooled girls I've interviewed have echoed these statements. They have talked about trusting themselves, pursuing their own goals, maintaining friendships even when their friends differ from them or disagree with them." Finally, these home-educated girls maintain their self-confidence as they pass into womanhood.[35]

Sheffer's findings regarding adolescent girls might explain some of the successes that other researchers have found regarding young adults who were home-schooled. In a study that categorized college students as either home, public, or private schooled, and examined their aptitude for and achievement in college English, the researchers found that "the home schooled students in this study demonstrate similar academic preparedness for college and similar academic achievement in college as students who had attended conventional schools."[36]

ACT and SAT tests are the best-known test predictors of success in university or college in America. The ACT publisher reported the scores of 1,926 home-schooled students from the high school graduating class of 1997. According to statistical rules of thumb, they outperformed the national average in English, reading, and on the overall composite of the ACT, while there was little to no difference in reasoning skills.[37]

The SAT scores of 5,663 homeschooled students across the United States were reported for the 1999–2000 school year. The home-educated who were on their way to university scored an average of 568 in verbal while the state school national average was 501, and 532 in math while the state school average was 510.[38] Increased research will soon reveal more of the significance of these results on the potential success of homeschooled students in higher education.

Paulo Oliveira and his colleagues found: "Although the [college] students who were educated in home schools had a slightly higher overall mean critical thinking score . . . than that of students who were from public schools, Christian schools, and ACE schools, the [statistical] . . . test revealed that there were no significant differences among the groups on this critical thinking score."[39]

Researchers in another study used academic, cognitive, spiritual, affective-social, and psychomotor criteria for measuring success at a private university. Among other things, they found that students who had been homeschooled held significantly more positions of appointed and spiritual leadership, and had more semesters of leadership service than did those from private schools, and were statistically the same as the public school graduates.[40]

Although some college and university personnel have shown animosity, and even hostility, toward the homeschooling process, it appears that most are now interested in welcoming the home-educated. Over 750 colleges and universities now admit home-educated students, and the list is growing fast. A nationwide survey of college admissions personnel revealed that "home schoolers are academically, emotionally, and socially prepared to succeed in college."[41]

Several colleges think so well of home-educated students that they have been actively recruiting them for several years. Another survey of college admissions officers found the Dartmouth College admissions officer saying, "The applications [from home schoolers] I've come across are outstanding. Home schoolers have a distinct advantage because of the individualized instruction they have received."[42]

This individualized instruction, combined with homeschooled students' experience in studying and pursuing goals on their own, is starting to show long-lasting effects. Admission officers at Stanford University think they are seeing an unusually high occurrence of a key ingredient, which they term "intellectual vitality," in homeschool graduates. They link it to the practice of self-teaching prevalent in these young people, as a result of their homeschool environment.[43]

J. Gary Knowles was the first to focus research on older adults who were home educated, collecting extensive data from a group who were home educated an average of about six years before they were 17 years old. He found that they tended to be involved in occupations that are entrepreneurial and professional, that they were fiercely independent, and strongly emphasized the importance of family. Furthermore, they were glad they had been home-educated, would recommend homeschooling to others, and had no grossly negative perceptions of living in a pluralistic society.[44]

A recent major nationwide study by researcher Brian D. Ray offers more insights, consistent with Knowles's findings, on home-educated adults. Chapter 2 of this book gives much detail on Ray's study, *Home Educated and Now Adults: Their Community and Civic Involvement, Views About Homeschooling, and Other Traits*.[45] In summary, 7,306 adults who had been homeschooled participated. Most of the findings reported were about the 5,254 who had been homeschooled for 7 or more years. In essence, they were very positive about their homeschool experiences, actively engaged in their local communities, keeping abreast of current affairs, highly civically involved, tolerant of others' expressing their viewpoints, religiously active but wide-ranging in their worldview beliefs, holding worldview beliefs similar to those of their parents, and largely home educating their own children.[45] The degree of the community and civic involvement supports some ideas that were expressed about homeschoolers about a decade earlier by Patricia Lines, formerly a researcher with the United States Department of Education. She asked whether homeschooling parents and their children are withdrawing from the larger public debate about education and, more generally, from social discourse that is an integral part of a liberty-loving republic. In a sense she addressed whether these children and youth are being prepared to be a significant part of society. Lines concluded:

> Although [homeschool parents] have turned their backs on a widespread and hallowed practice of sending children to a school located in a particular building, adhering to a particular schedule and program, they have not turned their backs on the broader social contract as understood at the time of the Founding [of the United States]. . . . Like the Antifederalists, these homeschoolers are asserting their historic individual rights so that they may form more meaningful bonds with family and community. In doing so, they are not abdicating from the American agreement. To the contrary, they are affirming it."[46]

Scott Schofield

I was homeschooled for grades three through 12. My mother and father have been deeply involved with our state's homeschool organization, which allowed me to participate in the larger homeschool community in the state and nationwide: helping at convention, working with and getting to know leaders, and so forth.

In my case, homeschooling was like putting a fish into water. It suited me. It allowed me to work at my own pace. I learned to read when I was three, so when the kindergarten teacher at school would point to the "a," and the class would respond "Aaaaah," I was bored. Once we began homeschooling, my strengths were used and my weaknesses worked on. There was only one time that I wanted to try public school. When I entered the junior high age . . . I envied the locker system. I had my own shelf at home, but lockers are cool, right?

As I grew up, I had few friends of my own age, and there were times that I really wanted that to change. But now, looking back, homeschooling was the right thing. My best friends were my brother, my mom, and my dad, and I enjoyed friendships with relatives, neighbors, and family friends of a variety of ages. I spent a great deal of my time with my own family, and I learned from them. The wisdom of my parents is worth much more than that of 29 other fourth graders. And now my brother remains my best friend. In retrospect, at age 22, I am very glad that I was homeschooled.

When I began homeschooling, one of the most common questions people asked was, "What about socialization?" A child grows up to be what he is taught and what he experiences. Parents often send their children off to sit under the tutelage of someone whom they barely know, to be taught that theories are facts and vice versa. The children then spend the rest of their day playing with and talking to children of roughly the same maturity level and often substandard morals. We live in an age in which children are committing such serious crimes that we often charge them as adults, but people do not seem to see a connection between children spending all day at a metal detector-controlled, government-run school, and the soaring crime rate among children.

Why not do bad things!? A person is affected by his surroundings. If a child is raised with drunks to believe that drinking is fine, that is what he will think. If a child hangs out with drug users, it is likely he will also use drugs. Peer pressure is strong, but the good news is that it works both ways; your children will learn from you if they hang around you all day. Through homeschooling, you have the opportunity to instill your moral values in your children.

It has now been four years since I graduated from the 12th grade, and my homeschooling experience continues to be of use. A couple of years ago, I earned a master's degree in business administration, largely by studying at home. I am currently working in the world of radio broadcasting. I write and edit news for the morning news show at a local radio station and do some news reporting. I also host the first half of the morning news. Just as it has helped me to this point, I know my years of home-schooling will help me with whatever I do in the future.

■　■　■

Similar to Lines' findings, Charles Clark's anecdotal report confirmed that home educators, who are models for their children, are involved in vigorous legislative lobbying.[47] Others have also discussed how home educators and their children receive an alternative education while staying involved in the larger political and social processes of America.

In a survey examining the rate at which parents are engaged in public civic activities, based on the method of schooling their children, the researchers used data from the 1996 National Household Education Survey conducted by the U.S. Department of Education, which differentiates between students educated in public, Catholic, non-Catholic church-related, and nonreligious private schools, and homeschooled students. Christian Smith and David Sikkink asked parents about the extent of family involvements in a variety of civic activities and concluded:

> Far from being privatized and isolated, home schooling families are typically very well networked and quite civically active. The empirical evidence is clear and decisive: private schoolers and home schoolers are considerably more civically involved in the public square than are public schoolers, even when the effects of differences in education, income, and other related factors are removed from the equation. Indeed, we have reason to believe that the

organizations and practices involved in private and home schooling, in themselves, tend to foster public participation in civic affairs . . . the challenges, responsibilities, and practices that private schooling and home education normally entail for their participants may actually help reinvigorate America's civic culture and the participation of her citizens in the public square.[48]

Ray's recent study of home-educaated adults clearly supports the idea that the role of modeling of home-school parents in the area of civic involvement is positivel correlated with the behavior of their home-educated adult children. That is, adults who were home educated are very active in the public square, as Smith and Sikkink found their parents are. The research to date suggests that the home educated are doing well in adulthood.[49]

Are They Becoming Technologically Literate?

The answer appears to be an implicit resounding yes. Research that has implicitly addressed the computer literacy of the home-educated has revealed these facts:

- Parents are "armed to the teeth with educational materials and technology. They all have computers and use them."[50]
- Eighty-six percent of the families in a nationwide study had a computer in their home, and computers were used for the education of children in 84 percent of these families.[51] By

FIGURE 8
STATE-APPROVED TEACHER CERTIFICATION NEEDED? HOMESCHOOL VERSUS STATE SCHOOL TEST SCORES

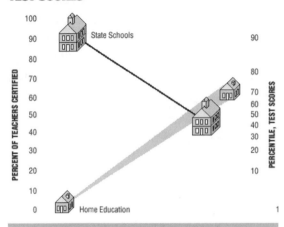

comparison, only about 34 percent of all United States families owned computers at the time. An even higher percentage of homeschool families in a more recent state-specific study had computers in their homes, and 61 percent of them were using the Internet for the education of their children.[52]

Limited research and news reports suggest that homeschoolers commonly use technology, including computers, the Internet, and distance-education courses, and that available technology will significantly increase the numbers of families homeschooling in America.[53]

* based on Ray '97
© 2002 Brian D. Ray. Figure used by permission.

Do the Children of Well-Educated or Certificated Parents Do Better in Homeschooling?

A number of researchers have explored whether the academic achievement of the home-educated is related to selected variables that might be of particular interest to policymakers and others. One of these factors of interest is whether the parents are government-certified teachers (Figure 8). Studies in Alabama, Oklahoma, Pennsylvania, Texas, nationwide twice, and nationwide in Canada all revealed that there was no significant relationship between student achievement and the teacher certification status of their parents (Figure 9).[54] Steven Duvall and his colleagues, on two occasions, have found that even special-needs children were successfully home-educated by parents who were not certified teachers.[55] One study in Montana found that whether the father was a certified teacher was not significant but that the mother's certification status was significant.[56] Richard Medlin, likewise, found a weak relationship between achievement and whether the mother was a certified teacher.[57]

The educational attainment of parents is another factor that is of interest to policymakers and some researchers. Several studies found no relationship between parents' educational attainment and the academic achievement scores of their home-educated children in Texas, Alabama, Oklahoma, and nationwide (Figure 10).[58] Others have found weak to moderate relationships between parents' formal educational attainment and their children's achievement

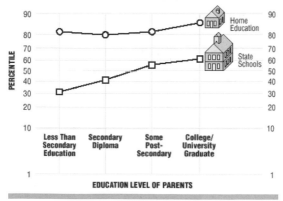

* based on Ray, 1997, Strengths of Their Own
© 2002 Brian D. Ray. Figure used by permission.

scores.[59] Even with these correlations, which do not necessarily indicate a causal relationship, the home-educated—even of parents with lower formal education—still tended to score above average on achievement tests.

Is There a Relationship Between Family Income and Success in Homeschooling?

Within the general, conventionally schooled population, it has been observed: "The children of parents who earn more money tend to do better than those where the parents earn less."[60] Policymakers and researchers have therefore been curious to discover whether the same holds true among homeschooling families. Several studies in this area have found:

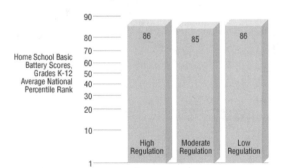

FIGURE 11.1
DOES GOVERNMENT (STATE) REGULATION IMPROVE HOMESCHOOL ACHIEVEMENT?

STATE REGULATION: No impact on homeschool achievement*

Home School Basic Battery Scores, Grades K-12 Average National Percentile Rank

High Regulation	Moderate Regulation	Low Regulation
86	85	86

*Based on data from Ray, 1997b.
© 2002 Brian D. Ray. Figure used by permission.

FIGURE 11.2

DOES GOVERNMENT (STATE) REGULATION IMPROVE HOMESCHOOL ACHIEVEMENT?

BREAKDOWN OF STATES BY REGULATORY POLICY

LOW REGULATION
No state requirement for parents to initiate any contact with the state.

MODERATE REGULATION
State requires parents to send notification, test scores, and/or professional evaluation of student progress.

HIGH REGULATION
State requires parents to send notification or achievement test scores and/or professional evaluation, plus other requirements (e.g. curriculum approval by the state, teacher qualifications of parents, or home visits by state officials).

*Based on data from Ray, 1997b.
© 2002 Brian D. Ray. Figure used by permission.

- No significant relationship exists between family income and student achievement in homeschool studies done in North Dakota, in most comparisons in an Oklahoma study, in Washington, and in one nationwide study.[61]
- Weak relationships between income and test scores in Washington and in a nationwide study.[62]

Note, however, that even with these weak correlations, which do not necessarily indicate a causal relationship, the home-educated tended to score above average.

Other Matters on Academic Achievement of Interest to Researchers and Policymakers

Should homeschooling be regulated more heavily by the state? Research to date has shown little to no relationship between degree of regulation by the state and students' academic achievement (Figures 11.1 & 11.2).[63] Parents are doing well with their children without government intervention.

Is the money spent on home education related to student achievement? Research findings suggest there

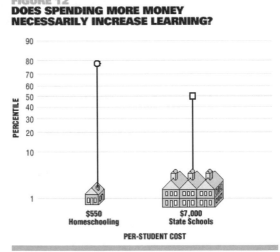

FIGURE 12
DOES SPENDING MORE MONEY NECESSARILY INCREASE LEARNING?

© 2002 Brian D. Ray. Figure used by permission.

is little to no relationship (Figure 12).[64] That is to say, homeschool students whose parents do not spend as much on their education tended to score above average on achievement tests even in the one study that found a relationship.

Various researchers have studied many factors and their relationships to the academic achievement of the home-educated. The next figure provides a summary of these relationships (Figure 13). Keep in mind that a statistical relationship does not necessarily establish

RELATIONSHIP BETWEEN VARIOUS INDEPENDENT VARIABLES AND ACADEMIC ACHIEVEMENT TEST SCORES OF HOME SCHOOL STUDENTS

This is a summary of the findings of many representative studies.

Factor Studied	Related to Academic Achievement in Home Schooling?
Money Spent on Education	No Relationship
Family Income	No Relationship Most Studies; a few studies found weak positive
Degree of State Regulation	No Relationship
Legal Status of Family	Typically No; one study found underground performed better
Father's Formal Education Level	Mixed Results; some slight positive
Mother's Formal Education Level	Mixed Results; some slight positive
Father Been Certified Teacher	Typically No Relationship; few studies found weak positive
Mother Been Certified Teacher	Typically No Relationship; few studies found weak positive
Gender of Student	No Relationship
Years Student Home Educated	Typically No Relationship; few studies slight positive
Time Spent in Formal Instruction	No Relationship
Age Began Formal Instruction	No Relationship
Use of Libraries	Typically No Relationship; occasional slight positive
Use of Computer	Typically No Relationship; occasional slight positive
Who Administered Test to Student	Typically No Relationship; occasional slight

cause and effect. The research is clear that children and youth who are home-educated are doing well in terms of academic achievement.

Does Homeschooling Help with Transmitting Values, Beliefs, and Worldview?

The limited research done on this factor to date suggests the answer is yes. In a preceding chapter, the reasons for parent-led home-based education were explained. One of the fundamental reasons is to transmit to children and youth a carefully chosen set of values, beliefs, and way of seeing the world. Tracy Romm studied homeschoolers in Atlanta, Georgia, and found some fascinating things.[65] For example, he concluded:

- "In summary, in all of these families the cultivation of strong character traits is viewed as the central goal of the home schooling effort."
- These parents, ". . . representing a variety of ideologies and motivations, are concerned primarily with the character-building function of education. As used here, character refers to religious or moral traits and to mental abilities that serve to preserve the distinctive qualities of each individual child. Schools are rejected as the referent for this process; they are viewed as serving more as a force for social conformity than as a protector of individual integrity."

For those who promote biblical values and a Christian worldview with their children, the evidence available to date suggests that homeschooling is an effective way to teach these things. Work by the Nehemiah Institute compares the thinking and worldview of students attending public, private, and home-based education. To date, they have found that the homeschooled are stronger in their biblical thinking regarding topics of politics, economics, education, religion, and social issues.[66]

Since values, beliefs, character, and worldview are so important to most homeschoolers, many hope to see more research done in this area. In other words, how well do their positive beliefs and behaviors persist into adulthood?

CHAPTER 5

How Homeschooling Affects the Family and Parents

The academic and social successes of homeschooled students are becoming well-known throughout much of society. This is true in nations such as the United States and Canada and increasingly the case in other nations such as Australia and Japan. In America, for example, the homeschooled are winning national spelling and geography bees and showing up on the cover of national newsmagazines. One even traveled with soon-to-be President George W. Bush in his campaign airplane because his mother worked for Mr. Bush. Multiple research reports and media stories have documented their general success in the basics of reading, writing, and arithmetic, and other academic disciplines. Fewer opponents of parent-led education are raising the socialization question, as research continues to document evidence that the homeschool environment and children are socially and emotionally healthy, while the state school environment and students more often are not.

Most young parents know that having children forces them, if they have not already done so, to clarify their beliefs, including those concerning child training practices and how children should be educated.

Considering and practicing homeschooling causes parents to think about their own educational experiences, evaluate available alternatives, change their relationships with their children, critically analyze societal norms, and learn anew or improve their knowledge of academic subjects. They must be willing to change fundamentally if they want to be the best possible parents and teachers of their children.

Togetherness, Camaraderie, and Cohesiveness

> "Our children enjoy being with their parents and are not 'ashamed' to be together as a family."
> —A homeschooling parent.[1]

Less publicized than the above issues, however, is how homeschooling affects family relationships and the parents themselves. One of the five top reasons given for homeschooling in places such as Canada and the United States is to build strong family ties. People in many western nations are tired of seeing the created natural family—the fundamental building block of a healthy society—crumble. And advocates of the life of the natural family—from around the world—are concerned that such disintegration is on its way to their nations.[2] They recognize that children and youth spend more time in a relationship with television, recorded music, and films than in meaningful relationships with their parents. They spend more time with peers than with their parents. They frequently spend more time talking with schoolteachers than with their fathers. The historically new generation gap has become an established fact, but perhaps not an immutable fact. The children's best friends are their classmates rather than their brothers and sisters.

Many of today's middle-aged parents began recognizing in the early 1980s that something was amiss with this picture of family life. They knew that there was something they wanted today that existed back in the "good old days." Regardless of whether their picture of the past was perfectly accurate or not, they knew they wanted healthier, richer, deeper, and stronger relationships within their families than they might have experienced growing up in the 1960s and 1970s and that they saw surrounding them in the 1980s. Homeschooling offers, to many such parents, one real, tangible, and promising way to reach their goal of growing stronger families.

One 41-year-old homeschooling father said it this way: "Not only are we moving away [from schools] but are moving *to* something. It's not just education; it's a way of life—a style, a family structure."[3] One researcher found that 36 percent of the homeschooling parents she studied said "they were satisfied with home schooling because it allows the parent and child to develop a close relationship which includes being able to see the 'light go on' when the child catches on to a concept being taught. The comments related to the close parent/child relationship indicated parents know they are meeting the child's social, spiritual, and educational needs in the best way possible."[4] Furthermore, the researcher found that 20 percent of parents listed family unity as a satisfying part of the homeschool experience.

Another researcher concluded: "All of the mothers felt homeschooling created a positive family relationship and strengthened the family unit."[5] Jon Wartes, head counselor at a public state high school, researcher, and homeschooling father, quoted one homeschool parent this way: "I think the main benefit too is the cohesiveness of our family unit. My son said yesterday, 'Mom, I appreciate all that you do for me . . . and I love you.' The children know you are really 'for them' and that you are sacrificing for them."[6]

Sociologist Allan Carlson explains how social forces that take activities and functions, such as education, out of the home and family, have had a destructive effect on the health of families, and therefore on children and nations: "The autonomous household bears the obligation and natural power to transmit to children the spiritual doctrines and beliefs of the family, the customs and folkways by which the household lives, the practical skills necessary for the later creation of new households, and the knowledge required for successful engagement in the world of commerce."[7] The structure and interaction patterns of homeschooling families are stronger in both cohesion and adaptability than in the general population of families with school-age children in institutional school settings. They have been able to achieve a dynamic equilibrium between stability and change, indicating that there are stabilizing forces within homeschool family systems not present in families that put their children in conventional school settings.[8]

Researcher Ronald Page concluded: "The effects of home schooling on the development of the family appear to be that the individual members of the family unit are more strongly bonded together, the father is drawn much more deeply into the whole life of the family, and the mother finds real fulfillment in her wider role. Within this [group of homeschoolers] . . . it would be no exaggeration to say that the impact upon the mother appears to be very considerable indeed."[9]

Gary and Jeanne Hodgson Family

Eleven years ago we "did what it takes" to homeschool our children. Jeanne was doing product development work; she quit her job. Gary became the family's sole source of financial support. We had no idea whether we could educate three children (or even survive) on his income as a route salesman. God has blessed us in our decision and continually has provided for our needs.

As young parents, we didn't know how satisfying it would be to see the loving friendships that our children (now ages 16, 14, and 12) have for one another. And although these close relationships weren't our primary reason for homeschooling, they have been significantly strengthened by having the family at home. In fact, as our children have grown, we've become aware that we haven't just taught social skills; by keeping our family together, we've built relationships. Furthermore, it is our hope that those relationships will be the foundation for a strong relationship with God (3 John 4).

So now, apart from the foundation, why do we continue in this tremendous effort to home educate? Gary and I, believing that we are loved and forgiven by the

God who created us, want to live for the purpose of giving glory to Him. Consequently, our entire focus, in fact our whole purpose, in raising children is to raise them in such a way that they are able to glorify and bring praise to the God who loves them more than we do. Therefore, since our purpose for educating differs radically from that of the state, we need to teach the children at home.

We are very aware that as we homeschool we are being evaluated by concerned friends and relatives. We do sometimes share the worry that our children may not be adequately prepared for college or university, should they choose to attend. However, we have clearly seen God's hand directing the children. God has provided for us, and we trust Him fully for the future.

■　■　■

Parents—the Adults in the Family—Learn Too

Obviously, there is mounting evidence that homeschooling has a positive effect on family health and family ties. What are its effects, however, on the parents themselves?

As they homeschool, parents grow to see themselves as proactive citizens in the realm of raising up children, the next generation of adults. They are a daily and important part of their children's lives, teaching them and watching the excitement in their eyes when they have a flash of insight or understanding. Most importantly, as they teach their sons and daughters, they are able to express and pass on their own values. At the same time, they learn along with their children.

Homeschoolers constantly talk about the new things they are learning, or finally understanding, that either they were never taught or understood in their conventional school days.[10] The excitement about learning is infecting the current generation of adults—as these comments demonstrate:[11]

- "I feel that my weak area, grammar, has been and is being greatly strengthened. . . . I have been relearning along with [my son]."
- "I've learned about our government and the constitution—some positive things and some negative."
- "How I hated [history] in school. It consisted of memorizing dates and facts and didn't seem to have any relation to anything. I just couldn't tie it all together! So now I am relearning this subject, and I find it fascinating! We have made a time line. I can finally see where everything goes and how it relates. We read interesting books—biographies and a good general text as well."
- "[We are learning about] the rich Christian heritage of America and a lot of historical truth that was ignored in my high school and college history classes."
- "When reviewing science, I am relearning and learning new information of the last 20-plus years."

It is often the case that other parents want to start homeschooling—after talking with an enthusiastic homeschool parent—so that they can finally learn all

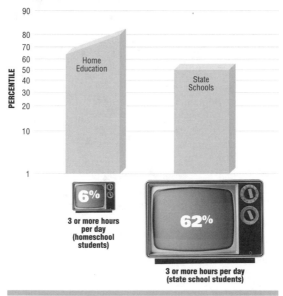

*Based on Ray, 1997, Strengths of Their Own
© 2002 Brian D. Ray. Figure used by permission.

the things they were supposed to learn in school, as well as the things they have always wanted to learn.

Family Culture Is Honored and Passed Along

Parents want to pass along to their children the uniqueness of their family history, their descendants, their roots, as it were. The Baker family. The Gomez family. The Schmidt family. The Liao family. The Suzuki family. Nationality, culture, ethnicity, faith, occupation, worldview, personality, and more are the creative details that comprise a particular family and its history.

In homeschooling, parents and family are clearly the main factors, the main forces that build up, impinge upon, and bring along each child (Figure 14). This family building, respect for roots, honoring of history, and hope for the future are not left to the workers in an institutional setting. At best, these workers may be part of a caring but nonfamily private company (private institutional school) that does its best to honor the family's character. On the other hand, these workers may be part of an impersonal government bureaucracy that regularly undermines or contradicts the family's character and cherished beliefs. By homeschooling, parents, family, siblings, grandparents, and persons who support and promote the family's beliefs and traditions are able to have purposeful and positive accomplishment in a home-educated child's or youth's life. These parents want to be a consequential, everyday part of their children's lives.

Research continues to show that a main reason for homeschooling is the parents' strong desire to transmit to their children carefully chosen familial, philosophical, religious, and cultural values, traditions, and beliefs, and a particular worldview.[12]

A FIRST-PERSON PROFILE

David and Shirley Quine Family

Shirley and I have nine wonderful children. We were blessed to be introduced to homeschooling before any of our children were of school age. We have been teaching our children at home for more than 25 years. We can honestly say that each year is a new adventure full of rich and exciting experiences.

Because we wanted to prepare our children to understand many of the thoughts and ideas of Francis Schaeffer, we set out three primary goals for our children:

- to know, love, and serve the Lord;
- to reason from the biblical worldview; and
- to challenge the false ideas of the secular culture with the Truth of Christianity.

Our nine children are truly a blessing. They range in age from 26 to nine. Bryce (26), our oldest, has recently graduated from Wake Forest Law School and is working in Dallas. Ben (24), is studying classical piano at the Lizst Academy in Budapest, Hungary, as a Fulbright Scholar. Betsy (21) has studied classical ballet. Blaine (21) is pursuing a career in classical ballet. Blessing (18) is a senior in high school and has interests in photography and sign language. Byron (14) is preparing himself for a possible career in engineering and aviation. Bethany (13) loves to study about and care for horses. She hopes to live on a horse ranch someday. Bonney (11) is our little artist, and Brett (9) is our singer and actor. Though we do not know the specific plans our loving Heavenly Father has for each of our children, we do know that they are plans to prosper them and to give them a hope and a future.

Mothers have often asked us, "What is the most difficult situation you have had to deal with?" Our oldest son Bryce did not read until he was almost 12 years old! We tried just about everything, but nothing seemed to work for him. Finally, we agreed that he would read when he was ready and until that time we would read to him as much as possible. What a joy that brought to him and to us. Making this decision led him to have a deep love of literature. The first three books he read were *The Lord of the Rings* trilogy.

Parents must see homeschooling as discipleship. There is no greater opportunity, and there is no greater privilege. We are to teach, to guard, to guide, and to tend them. Our children will become the "letter of Christ . . . known and read by all men" as described in 2 Corinthians 3. We must be equipping them to reason from the biblical worldview so that they will always be ready to give a reasoned defense to anyone who asks them to explain the hope they have in Christ (1 Pet. 3:15).

Though academically homeschooling is superior, we believe that its greatest benefit is the reestablishment of the family. The relationships that develop, the closeness that results, and the commitment that our family has to one another are truly the greatest rewards for Shirley and me.

In addition to homeschooling our own children, Shirley and I founded the Cornerstone Curriculum Project in 1984. It is our greatest desire to assist parents disciple their children. I have written educational materials in math, science, art, music, and an integrated high school curriculum teaching the worldviews of the Western world.

Contact: David and Shirley Quine, Cornerstone Curriculum Project, 2006 Flat Creek Place,

Richardson, TX 75080, tel. 972–235–5149, www.cornerstonecurriculum.com.

■ ■ ■

Parents Grow—as Adults, as Parents, and as Citizens

Parents find that when they homeschool they become dynamic participants in building family unity and strengthening the family as an important social institution. "There is *direct* evidence of a *strong* linkage between the *spread* of mass state education and the *decline* of the family."[13] Many parents report that, when they homeschool, they can see their family renewed and strengthened, especially if they once had their children in institutional schools. Their adult and parental strength and competence are increased when they decide to continue the care, upbringing, and education of the children they began to care for at conception. This ongoing assumption of responsibility is both heartening and empowering for parents.

A current sociopolitical move in nations all around the world has devalued the role of parents and exalted the role of society and government in raising children. This philosophy is embodied in a newly popular African proverb: "It takes a village to raise a child." Kay Cole James, herself an African-American, points out three fundamental problems with this African proverb: "First, children do not belong to the *village* or to the community or to the government. They belong to parents, and the *village* exists as a resource for these families. Second, even if we did believe this proverb to be true, the *village* no longer exists. And third, what the *village* liberals seek to build is, in truth, simply big government."[14]

When using this maxim, the village liberals are not seeking to build the sound, traditional family as history has known it. As one homeschooling parent remarked: "I've learned we are qualified to teach and guide our own children. That no one cares for your child and his future more than you."[15]

Homeschooling keeps parents responsible to their God-ordained duty. "I have learned that we do not need to turn our kids over to the 'experts' because we, as parents, are the experts. God intended for parents to participate in every aspect of their children's growing up experience."[16] In describing the unfortunate relationship between modern state (public) schools and parents, Eric Buehrer made the fascinating comment that state schools are to parents what codependents are to alcoholics.[17] That is, the schools increasingly enable parents to abandon their natural responsibilities, as they hand their children over to the schools. This exchange of parental responsibilities between public schools and families snowballs. Yet the homeschooling parent (unlike the alcoholic, who is enabled by a codependent to continue in his irresponsible behavior) is able to continue or retrieve his important position of responsibility in his or her children's lives.

These parents are not passively sitting by in their kitchens, either. They are out making a difference in the political and social world. Daniel Golden, a reporter for the *Wall Street Journal*, recently investigated the political activities of homeschool parents. He reported:

> "When I started home-schooling, I was worried that we were withdrawing from society," says another [lobbying] trainee, Jo Hershy [homeschool parent] of Lancaster, Pennsylvania. "But now I feel we have the best of both worlds. We home-school, and we influence educational policy nationwide." Do they ever. Although often portrayed as an isolated fringe group, parents who teach their children at home have become inside-the-Beltway pros, wielding enough clout to help block a Clinton administration bid for national student testing, launch their own political action committee and push their concerns into the midst of this year's presidential race. Despite relatively small numbers . . . their ability to overwhelm Congress and state legislatures with phone calls, faxes, e-mails and visits has won them a unique status as educational conscientious objectors."[18]

For some adults, just a little political involvement is a big change in their lives. One homeschool parent reported: "I've become more interested and a little involved in politics because of our concern for children and family."[19]

In a similar vein, Patricia Lines, while working for the United States Department of Education, wrote:

Although [home school parents] have turned their backs on a wide-spread and hallowed practice of sending children to a school located in a particular building, adhering to a particular schedule and program, they have not turned their backs on the broader social contract as understood at the time of the Founding [of the United States]. . . . Like the Antifederalists, these homeschoolers are asserting their historic individual rights so that they may form more meaningful bonds with family and community. In doing so, they are not abdicating from the American agreement. To the contrary, they are affirming it."[20]

Parents who decide to stay home and teach their children find themselves being true to what they know to be right. Researchers and parents know that many of the arrangements in modern society that place children for more time with other than their parents and at home put the children at risk. Risks include problems related to:

- physical health, such as ear infections, gastrointestinal disease, and other communicable diseases;
- behavioral disorders, such as ADD, ADHD, and violence;
- psychological health problems, including anxiety and depression; and
- family breakdown: the drawing away from parents and siblings.

For examples of these and other risks, see almost any issue of the journal *New Research*, which monthly chronicles new research related to the family.[21]

Parents' Hearts Are Turned Toward Their Children

Many people think that parents choose to homeschool their children because the parents' hearts are interested in their children and because they desire to invest much of themselves in their children. This is true for many homeschool parents. It is also true, however, that by choosing proactively to take on the role of main educators of their children rather than send them away to others, parents find themselves increasingly interested in their children's lives. They want to invest more in them. They desire to spend more time with them and to give more of themselves to them.

An old saying says, "For where your treasure is, there will your heart be also."[22] In other words, parents find that their hearts are for their children once they choose to put treasure (such as time, interaction, care) in them. And this is good, since it is always good when the hearts of fathers and mothers turn toward their children and the hearts of the children turn to their fathers and mothers.[23]

Whether it is because parents have read about the risks, heard friends testify to the risks, have experienced the problems with their own children, or are somehow endowed with an innate parental sense, they know they should spend more time with their children. In fact, researchers have found that many parents think they should stay home to take care of their children but lie to themselves as they develop rationales for why they go to work and do not stay home.[24] Homeschooling does not cure all the problems regarding parent-child relationships, but it does help many parents to do what they know to be right in raising their children.

A PROFILE

Mary Kay Clark, Ph.D.

Mary Kay Clark has taken an active role in educational and political issues for over 30 years. Seeing firsthand the opportunities and the pitfalls of private schooling, Clark left a private academy and began teaching her children at home. She emphasizes that through the ages, the popes have referred to the home as the "domestic church." It is in this church of the home that the Roman Catholic faith is learned and lived. Home education makes parents the primary educators of their children—not only in name but in deed, teaching them by word and example the Christian life of love and sacrifice. In the home, children learn virtue along with their mathematics. They learn self-control along with their reading. They learn patience along with science. Home education allows families to "become what they are," a little church in the home.

While in Ohio, Clark helped establish a private school, where she served as principal. Later in Ohio, she helped establish the state's private homeschooling association. Upon moving to Virginia in 1982, she helped found the Home Educator's Association of Virginia, for which she served as executive secretary for several years. Under her direction, Seton Home Study School, emphasizing Roman Catholic education, has grown from 340 students in 1985 to more than 10,000 currently enrolled in the United States and internationally. Seton Educational Media publishes Catholic curriculum materials for homeschoolers and private schools.

Clark earned a Ph.D. in education from Assumption University. She speaks at home education and family conferences and is a guest on radio and television programs. She has written many articles on homeschooling and the book *Catholic Home Schooling: A Handbook for Parents.* Clark is the mother of seven children, all of whom she has educated at home.

Contact: Seton Home Study School, P. O. Box 396, Front Royal, VA 22630, www.setonhome.org.

■ ■ ■

CHAPTER 6

How Homeschooling Affects Society

A standard belief in most societies is that well-educated adults make better adults. It is also usually thought that well-educated citizens make better citizens. If these two ideas are true, then any nation that encourages families to homeschool will also be an improved nation. That is because the evidence to date shows the home-educated perform better academically than do those in institutional state-run schools, on average.

It is also known that if *education* only refers to knowledge and understanding in subject areas (for example, math, writing, science), then it is possible to have a lot of well-educated fools and failures in society. That is, people who just have knowledge in their brains but lack wisdom, discipline, and right choices end up causing all kinds of problems and are not very happy or satisfied in life. At this point, it appears that home-schooling will produce wise adults who make good decisions, because their parents are modeling a lot of good things for them. For example, their parents are modeling:

- involvement, that is, time, in their children's lives;

- a high value placed on children and consequently human life;
- personal discipline and sacrifice;
- strong family relationships;
- long-lasting marriages;
- lifelong learning (by the parents);
- productivity, not just consumption; and
- freedom of thought and action in a just society.

A PROFILE

Patrick Farenga

Patrick Farenga is president of Holt Associates, Inc., and publisher of *Growing Without Schooling* magazine. He and his wife, Day, homeschool three daughters, ages 14, 11, and 8. He has been involved in the homeschooling movement since 1981, when he came to work at Holt Associates. Farenga worked closely with the late author and teacher John Holt from 1981 until Holt's death in 1985. Holt left the company to Farenga and a small board of directors to continue his work, often referred to as "unschooling."

Farenga's vision in homeschooling is to help adults and children live and learn together in their homes and local communities in ways that conventional schooling prevents or ignores. He believes, as Holt did, that our chief educational problem is not to make homes more like schools but to make schools less like schools. Farenga's most recent book is *The Beginner's Guide to Homeschooling*.

Farenga speaks about learning outside of school and conventional curricula at conferences throughout the world, writes for homeschooling and scholarly journals, and has appeared as a homeschooling expert on national TV and radio shows, including *The Today Show*, CNN's *Parenting Today*, and *The Voice of America*.

Contact: Patrick Farenga at Holt Associates/GWS, 2380 Massachusetts Ave. Suite 104, Cambridge, MA 02140, tel. 617-864–3100, toll-free ordering 888–925–9298, www.holtgws.com.

■ ■ ■

Time, Time, Time—Inexpensive but Priceless

Family breakdown. Generation gap. No time for each other. The phrases and concepts are so common that many people accept them as inevitable. The most obvious benefit of homeschooling may be the least noticed—and the most important. By its very nature, homeschooling makes it possible for parents and children to spend a lot of time together.

There is a popular American song from the 1970s called "The Cat's in the Cradle."[1] This ballad tells of a father who never took time to be with his son. The boy keeps asking his father to spend time with him, but the father continually says he cannot now but will take the time later. After the boy becomes a grown man, his aged father is sorely disappointed because his son has no time for him. In the end, the problem passes from one generation to the next. The song makes some of the most heartless men cry, especially fathers whose children are in their late teens and early twenties.

Many people have heard the astounding research finding that fathers in the United States, on average, spend very few minutes per day in any kind of meaningful interaction with their children. For mothers who work outside the home, the amount of time is probably not much more. Precious little time is spent together even when one parent is a homemaker. Parents who send their children away to institutional schools know that no matter how much time they think they should spend or want to spend with their children, the opportunity is very limited because children spend so much time at school and in school-related activities. A recent nationwide U.S. study found that 40 percent of fathers do not even know the name of their children's teachers. Also, 40 percent never read to their children, and another 11 percent read to them only once a month to once every three months.[2] It is difficult to understand why a father would not want to know the name of one of the most important persons in his child's life. Putting them in schools makes it even less likely that the parents will have careful knowledge of their lives.

Many of the in-school and school-related activities may be good in and of themselves, but reality dictates that time in these is largely time when parents and children are not together. Homeschool parents and children have about 53 percent more time available to be together than is the case when parents send their children away from home to institutional schools.

In addition, institutional schoolchildren and youth tend to focus their lives on their school peers, and their parents and siblings are less important to them than in homeschool families. In other words, when not in school during the school day, school students are more likely to spend even more time with their school peers.

The disparate amount of time available for a school student's family is an earth-shattering reality. Almost everyone in most developed nations knows that there is a tremendous disconnect between parents and children and between the older generation and the younger generation (i.e., the generation gap). Furthermore, it is also known that many children really do not care much to be with their own siblings, but no one seems to be able to do anything about these problematic predicaments. Homeschooling changes all this.

Children Are Valuable

Second, research makes it clear that homeschool parents place a high value on having children. In the U.S., they have just over three children per family, about 60 percent more children than the national average. And a relatively large percentage of them have large families with four to eight children. Limited data show the figures may be about the same in Canada and Germany. The simple and obvious fact that they decide to homeschool their children tells their children—as a matter of reality—that father and mother care about them. This enhances a child's security and success in life much more than do a television in every bedroom, another kitchen convenience, or a nicer home, for example.

Personal Discipline and Sacrifice

Reporters for the May 12, 1997, cover story of *U.S. News and World Report* pointed out that many parents are lying to themselves about why both the mother and father work outside the home.[3] They tell themselves lies: "We both work because we need the money." The data do not support this claim. At the same time, an increasing number of parents are deciding to home-school and are choosing to live on one income in order to be with and teach their children. They forgo the extra money and its attendant pleasures that they could have had by getting the second income. Again, this decision tells the children that they are extremely important to their parents while less important are new clothes (since those from second-hand stores are suffi-cient), movies at the theater (since rented videos for $1.99 for the whole family are sufficient), computer games (since old-fashioned board games are sufficient), more meals at fast-food restaurants (since home-cooked meals from scratch are sufficient), a second car, or a nicer apartment or house. They are modeling to their children discipline and sacrifice for higher values. These character traits will naturally benefit society in the long run.

Strong Family Relationships

Homeschool parents cite creating strong family rela-tionships as one of their main reasons for home-schooling. As described elsewhere in this book, research to date shows that homeschooling does actu-ally contribute to healthy families and strong ties between family members. Although there are many indications that an unfortunately large number of fam-ilies are weak and falling apart in some nations, most people still recognize that strong families clearly contribute to strong societies.

Parents spending both "quantity time" and "quality time" with their children is both the possibility and the reality in homeschooling. In addition, homeschooling creates an environment in which siblings are able to spend a good deal of time together. With proper teaching and good examples from the parents, the children and youth learn to become best and lifelong friends. These strong family relationships and sibling bonds will last into the future, even into these children's elderly years. These strong familial bonds are a significant advantage to those who have them during times of duress, stress, illness, loss, and other challenges. They provide both tangible and intangible benefits that government-sponsored programs can never provide.

Myriad research studies show that strong families—healthy bonds between parents and children and among siblings—result in improved academic achievement, fewer babies born out of wedlock, happier and healthier children and parents, higher income and standard of living, and many other benefits. The journal *New Research* (on the family) chronicles this research in almost every monthly issue.[4]

One homeschooling parent reports, "Our teen age daughter wants us to be her role models and closest friends, not her peers. Our relationship with her has been strengthened in a way I never thought possible."[5]

Homeschooling builds up the natural family's structure and strength. This is and will be one of its greatest contributions to the future of many nations.

Jesse and Arné Williams Family

We first heard about homeschooling from an interview on Focus on the Family's radio program. At the time we did not know of any African-American families, as we are, that homeschooled. Trying to explain to people why we were homeschooling was like trying to explain a spiritual concept to a carnal mind.

Public (state) school was not working for our son, our second child, and we started homeschooling him in the fourth grade. We could not have told you at the time—with any certainty—where that decision was taking us, but the effects are still working now, 14 years later.

Both of us graduated from Tuskegee Institute (University) in Alabama and come from families that place great value on education. Family members did not say much when we started homeschooling but offered their assistance where they could.

We would like to see the homeschool movement grow and influence the African-American community in a greater measure. It is alarming that the children are being labeled and placed in special programs that would limit their future success.

Shortly after we started homeschooling we founded Living Praise Worship Center and a school for home-schoolers. We believe homeschooling is the biblical way in which Christian children should be educated.

It is the year 2001, and it has been fourteen years. We have homeschooled three of our four children, and the two youngest will graduate in May. We homeschooled our second child through the 10th grade, after which he returned to public school to take part in the sports program. The greatest benefit has been to watch them grow in their Christian faith and become independent learners.

■ ■ ■

Long-Lasting Marriages

Homeschool parents model marital commitment to their children. In most homeschool families, the father and mother work together to develop, evaluate, and refine their educational philosophy and practice. Veteran homeschoolers think that the more parents work together, the more successful their homeschooling will be. The simple fact that their fathers and mothers are working together on this important endeavor presents to children one of the key ways a marriage should function.

Most married persons recognize that the more a husband and wife work together on common challenges and tasks, the more likely it is their marriage will endure. Homeschooling clearly gives them an important, common task. This author has heard many stories about how homeschooling has drawn husbands and wives together in a closer and healthier way.

Research clearly shows the benefits to children and youth of having married parents and the ill effects of divorce or single parenthood resulting from fornication. You will find evidence of this in almost any issue of the journal *New Research* (noted on previous pages), which monthly chronicles new research related to the family. Compared to the national average, a high percentage of homeschool families are headed by a married couple. This models for the children the importance of being married if one wants to have children and the importance of staying married.

This is not to say that single parents should not or cannot homeschool their children. On the contrary, many single parents—whether single because of the death of a spouse, divorce, or fornication—successfully home-educate their children. Regardless of marital status, homeschooling one's child sends a strong message to the child of the parent's love and concern. Such may not be possible if the child were sent to an institutional school.

Lifelong Learners

Most professional educators and most adults agree that it is a good thing to continue learning throughout one's lifetime. Homeschool parents are constantly modeling to their children that they like to learn and are continuing to learn. The very nature of their role as home educators defines them as learners. They read with their children, prepare lessons for their children, and often do extra study to keep one step ahead of their children in order to teach them something essential for their education.

As one homeschool parent explained it:

> I have learned that education is not found, necessarily, by completing a series of books. Instead, education is found by being interested

in the world around us, by being fascinated by people, places, and things. I began home-schooling because I wanted my kids to regard learning as a lifelong fun project. By being home, and with me when I am in town, or on a "field trip," *they* have taught *me* to enjoy people, to be curious about places and things. If they maintain this curiosity and pursuit of how, why, who, what, they will learn all their lives. Although this was my goal, I wasn't sure it was obtainable. Now I am sure. It *is* obtainable.[6]

A nation of lifelong learners is a nation of adult citizens reading, thinking, producing ideas, and paying attention to the philosophies and actions of government, business, and religious leaders. This makes for a stronger, more aware, involved, and productive citizenry.

Producers, Not Consumers

Choice in education, vouchers, charter schools, tuition tax credits, and more have been points of heated debate in the United States for about a decade. When some talk about "choice in education," they really mean a parent having a choice among several state-controlled (public) schools within a bus-ride's distance from a family's home. Others mean choice between state-run and private schools, while funding or subsidizing both types of schools with tax money. In all of these scenarios, the parents (or students) are clearly the consumers. They are out to shop for, evaluate, and buy something, though not necessarily with their own money. Many argue that a more free-market approach to schools offering their products (schooling) and parents (or students) choosing among competing providers will increase the quality of the product. In many ways, complete, unfettered, free-market schooling has not been allowed in America because of state schools' unequal control and influence over the funding and infrastructure of schooling. Regardless of this, the parents (or students) are kept in their roles as consumers.

Homeschooling changes all this. Parents and students who homeschool can become, essentially, producers. With respect to education, they produce their own vision, mission, dreams, curriculum goals and objectives, lesson plans, schedules, field trips, books, support groups, newsletters, and more. They do not have to sit by, passively awaiting the offering of some school that is run by formally trained school people. Research shows that about 75 percent of home-educating parents basically construct their own curriculum for their children.[7] The other 25 percent actively seek out, examine, evaluate, and choose from a host of available "complete curriculum packages." Even those who choose a package do so with great freedom and almost no control from any government agency. They are indeed free in many ways. Furthermore, the sense of productivity and personal capacity expands beyond the confines of just schooling, that is, academics.

Homeschooling is often the catalyst that gives both parents and children the urge to be entrepreneurial. In homeschooling, they learn that they can indeed be creative and benefit from their own creativity. Being in charge of their children's education increases the self-confidence of adults so that they are willing to come up with ideas and try running their own businesses. In a sense, homeschooling gives both the parents and children the idea that they are able to do things if they only set their minds to it.

Allan Carlson chronicles how, in Western nations, serious threats to the natural and traditional family have been imposed by industrial organization and the state. Furthermore, Carlson shows: "Meaningful family survival depends on the building and maintenance of a true household economy, one that exists apart from the national and international economies and that reconciles the claims of the dependent young, old, and sick with the abilities and obligations of those able to work."[8]

Others have also described how the Industrial Revolution converted large portions of women from being active producers to consumers.[9] Unfortunately, it was not only women who became more oriented to consumption. Changes during the middle 1800s led an increasing numbers of people from various social sectors to focus on what they could consume. Along with these changes, mass compulsory (compulsion) institutional schooling led more and more parents to believe that someone other than themselves should teach their children. Carlson explains how families who homeschool today can reclaim some of the good things—such as productive, home-based creativity and economies—that have been lost in modern cultures.[10]

In Australia, researcher John Barratt Peacock found that homeschool families were clearly becoming more creative and developing their own ways to produce items and services for their own families and for others. Fathers were learning skills so they could work from home and be with their children more. The mothers, fathers, and children were making more things (e.g., cheese, garments) for their own use and buying fewer things from stores.[11]

Families—both parents and children—who home-school are given the confidence that they can orient themselves more as producers and less as consumers. They are not sitting about waiting for corporations, political leaders, or government agencies to suggest to them what they need and want and should purchase and consume. They learn and then apprehend that they can act, produce, and be effective.

Freedom of Thought and Action in a Just Society

If you ask any youth or adult in the United States what makes America unique, many will respond that America is a free country. In other words, America is supposed to have freedom of thought, freedom of religion, freedom of expression, and freedom to do business. Many other nations, especially those that consider themselves democracies, also pride themselves in having significant freedom in these things.

Not all of what we have today is as simple as it may appear. Thomas Jefferson, who is thought of as one of the great freedom thinkers, "saw nothing wrong with indoctrinating students into a philosophy of government as long as it corresponded to his understanding of orthodoxy."[12]

Jefferson's contemporary, Benjamin Rush unabashedly predicted that "our schools of learning, by producing one general and uniform system of educator, will render the mass of the people more homogeneous and thereby fit them more easily for uniform and peaceable government."[13]

Two hundred years later, an American professor of education claimed, "Each child belongs to the state."[14]

Are the people in nations that consider themselves to be progressive and democratic free indeed? Of the concepts related to homeschooling, this may be the most difficult to consider. But the reader may ask how this question is related to homeschooling.

Consider this: In America, an astounding 87 percent of all school children are taught in state (public) schools. In other words, they are taught by employees of the state, the government. Public school teachers and administrators are agents of the state. Although the term *agent* may carry negative connotations, teachers in public schools are—in fact and in many ways—just that, representatives or ambassadors of the state. They teach only things that are approved by government authorities or a small group of citizens (and then approved by the state). They use only books approved by government authorities or a small group of citizens (and then approved by the state). They are prohibited from saying things that government authorities or laws that regulate public agencies do not allow to be said in government institutions. They must follow the dictates and controls of the state since they are representatives and employees of the state.

Here is the dilemma: If 87 percent of all children and youth are being taught by government-approved and government-controlled teachers who may only use government-approved and government-controlled textbooks, movies, and literature (that is, ideas), then how can anyone say the citizens and the nation as a whole are truly free? Parents are allowing the state to indoctrinate their children for at least 12 years of their lives (and many go for another 4 years in state-run university or college). These persons, taught in state-run schools for 12 or more years are eventually the voting citizens, leaders, and workers within the state. Does this practice encourage free thinking? Does it enhance creativity without significant government influence? Will the citizens truly be challenged to have a careful eye and critical mind that will vigilantly watch the government and hold it accountable to the nation's constitution and citizens' rights?

For example, during the vote-counting ordeal for the U.S. presidential election in the fall of 2000, most adult Americans had little understanding of the constitutional law and issues at stake. Is there any solid evidence that such heavy state involvement in the education of citizens nurtures the awareness of liberty that produced free countries like the United States of America in the first place? Many doubt it.

One homeschool parent found that by being the main provider of education for his children he learned "how politics works—how it affects the family."[15] Another parent was very blunt about the crux of the education of children and what he or she learned from homeschooling: "Social/political struggle of parents [versus] government in the homeschool arena is not a question of educational credentials, method or doctrine but *power* and who will control the future."[16] More are homeschooling, and they are a growing portion of those not in government schools (Figure 15).

Many advocates of state-run education want as many children and youth as possible to study in state-controlled schools. Relatively few of these state-school advocates will commit their thoughts to writing. One who has done so, Michael Apple, is a professor at a state university. He thinks that a large portion of

FIGURE 15
NUMBER OF HOMESCHOOL & PRIVATE SCHOOL STUDENTS IN THE U.S. (GRADE LEVELS K-12, ESTIMATED)

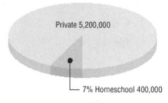

Private 5,200,000

7% Homeschool 400,000

1990-1991 TOTAL 5,600,000

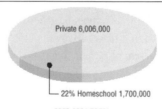

Private 6,006,000

22% Homeschool 1,700,000

2000-2001 TOTAL 7,706,000

Based on USDE/NCES 1999
© 2002 Brian D. Ray. Figure used by permission.

homeschoolers are "attacking" the state (government) and that when parents homeschool their own children it will probably hurt other parents' children or other "groups" of persons.[17] Apple makes these rather incredible and predictive claims without providing a factual foundation. Another critic of homeschooling, Chris Lubienski, also a professor at a state university, claims that homeschooling will hurt the "public good."[18] He does not think that if these millions of homeschool students worldwide are individually benefited that societies will necessarily be benefited. He argues that these parents and their children are basically "self-interested"—in other words, selfish. Again, these claims are made without a factual foundation or convincing logic. This book's readers may want to read Apple and Lubienski for themselves.

Many others, however, contradict the views of Apple and Lubienski.

For example, Patricia Lines, who formerly worked for the United States Department of Education and has studied homeschooling and known homeschool families since 1983 or earlier, does not think homeschoolers are selfish or ignoring public life. She observes: "Antifederalist or homeschooler, liberal or conservative, these people often demonstrate libertarian tendencies. Almost all are decentralists in one way or another. Like the vast numbers of Antifederalists, the vast numbers of homeschoolers assert their right to an inner sphere of conscience and privacy, but not for the sake of selfish individualism. They assert it for the sake of belonging to a community of their own choosing."[19]

In another context, I have identified positive effects of homeschooling. I have served as an instructor or professor at both state and private colleges and universities, and have worked in a private research institute. My research and experience have led me to believe that the positive effects of homeschooling on individual children and youth will clearly benefit the larger society.[20] In fact, research evidence continues to mount (as explained earlier in this book) that the academic, social, emotional, free-thinking, and family-life benefits of homeschooling are showing up in the lives of adults who were homeschooled. This, clearly, is having a positive effect on the "public good"—it can only do so.

In one of my research articles, I explain:

> Proponents of compulsory schooling law and state-controlled schools, whether "leftists" or "rightists," are working, perhaps unwittingly, to make sure that something called the "common curriculum"—the one approved by those in positions of power—is taught to all (or most) children. Advocates of these government institutions hope they will long be the ones in positions of power. Conversely, most proponents of home schooling and parental choice and authority only want to make sure that their personally chosen curriculum is taught to their children. These folks are not asking the state or anyone else for money or power to teach their curriculum to anyone else. They are asking the state and their neighbors to assume that they,

the parents, have the best interests of their children and society's common good in mind. In fact, these parents are only asking the state, and their neighbors and thinkers who empower and influence the agents of the state, to let them go about their lives peaceably and quietly in the privacy of their homes and communities with their children. Advocates of home-based education are familiar with the golden rule and the big issues of liberty and justice for all in society. These parents want the state to allow individual citizens to choose freely when and how they will help other parents.

Home schooling allows parents, in a context of nurture and high social capital, to choose freely a unique and effective education for their children. As a child grows older year by year, the parents and the child forge stronger bonds and a richer, relationally developed curriculum. Parents and children in such an arrangement, under no compulsion or coercion from the state, are allowed to escape the hidden curriculum of others and of the state, choose texts for learning, and work together in their communities as they "see work—family—religion—recreation—school as an organically related system of human relationships" . . .

The battles over power and domination that riddle state-run schools cannot sap home schooling parents and their children of their strength, consume their energy, and destroy their zest for learning. Zeal for social justice, liberty, the common good, and being right with one's Creator can be approached from an environment of security, strength, and stability while the ever-maturing child year after year steps out into larger and more expansive spheres of challenge, democratic deliberation, and creative service to others.

The voices of those who are anti-home schooling, anti-parents' rights, and antichoice and of those who assert that home schooling causes "balkanization," "divisiveness," "social anarchy," "narrow-mindedness," fundamentalism," "segregationism," and "possessive individualism" are increasingly hollow and impotent. Evidence supporting their claims is (and always has been) scarce to nonexistent . . . Furthermore—and tragically for this nation's children and to the chagrin of the proponents of state-run schools—the power struggles, illegal drug deals, racism . . . , violence, philosophical contention, religious censorship, lack of parent involvement, low academic achievement, high dropout rates, premarital sexual activities, teachers' and bureaucratic antiparental power . . . , and greed-based highstakes labor disputes that are associated with the halls and culture of public schools and so powerfully overshadow the significant incidents of success and joy therein make the common criticisms of parent-led home schooling look very wan and insignificant.[21]

There is good evidence that homeschooling is teaching children and youth to think for themselves, helping them do well in their academic subjects, showing them they can be successful without government subsidies and excessive state controls in their lives, and leading them to be active and productive family members and citizens.

A FIRST-PERSON PROFILE

Wes and Deborah Butler Family

My husband Wes, our seven children, and I are beginning our fifteenth year of homeschooling—a journey that began when our oldest went to public (state) kindergarten.

Our daughter cried every day. People said, "Oh, she needs to get used to it," so I hardened myself to thinking that I was just being too sensitive. She changed to a different teacher during the middle of the next year. She didn't mind school as much after that, but both the low quality of the teachers and the effects of her classmates made me nervous.

I decided to try what only one person I knew was doing—homeschooling. We were never again the same! We worked on attitudes that year—problems I hadn't noticed were sneaking in.

The next year I sent my two children again to school. My son didn't like it at all. "They never teach me anything new!" he often said. He hated school. My daughter, quickly turning into a "Valley Girl" before my eyes, and began despising her little brother. We decided to homeschool again! The principal at the school told me I could do a better job than they could. The children were excited about "school at home" and working on math in their pajamas!

After moving to Oregon, we tried the state schools for two weeks. We have homeschooled ever since. How could we have entrusted state schools—strangers—with such an important job as educating our children?

The more we homeschooled, the more I could see the benefits: our son became more outgoing each year; our children became best friends and liked to be together. They could entertain children and talk to senior citizens. Our family became very close. I calmed down.

I want to continue to train them up as Christians. I want to give them positive influences and keep them from bad influences as long as possible—pointing out the consequences of bad behavior. Since I now have two homeschool graduates, it is surprising how fast the time went. I have such a different perspective now! How could I ever have not wanted to spend the mornings and days with my precious children? They are fun to be with, quick learners, and very creative. They invent games to play and speak freely to all age groups. Homeschooling our children is one of my best experiences—endless work, but endlessly rewarding!

■　■　■

CHAPTER 7

I'm a Teenager and I Want to Homeschool

Are you a teenager in school and thinking any of these things?

- I'm bored.
- I hate my teachers; none of them care.
- I feel like I'm wasting my best years.
- I don't have time for what really interests me.
- I would like to go to a really good university and don't think I am being well prepared.
- I am tired of fighting constant pressure from other students in class.
- I am being told how to think and act all the time.
- My mom or dad could do better than that.
- I'm tired of the peer pressure—how to act, dress, talk, use drugs, do sex, rebel against my parents.
- I am fairly happy at school, but I could do more with my time at home.
- I just don't feel safe at school.
- I'd like to spend more time with my brothers and sisters and parents.
- I think that there are better ways I could express my faith, to be a witness for Christ.
- My teachers don't give me a chance to explain my views.

When my oldest child—the oldest of eight children—was first-grade age and being homeschooled, she really wondered what all the other children were doing in the local state (public) school. So her mom and I arranged with a first-grade schoolteacher for our daughter to attend school for a day. A little more than halfway through the day someone asked the seven-year-old whether she was enjoying the day. She responded, "I really liked recess" (play time outside). That evening, I asked her whether she would like to attend school, and she replied, "No, not really." "Why not?" I asked. "Because they are always sitting around doing nothing," came the quick reply. A remarkable answer considering that she had been in a well-managed classroom that was taught by a well-respected, likable, and state-licensed teacher.

Upon further discussion, I found out that she was disappointed by all the time waiting in lines (queues), the time wasted while the teacher had to settle small disputes and minor disruptions caused by students, time waiting for others to finish projects or assignments, and time watching a little boy stand in front of the class while attempting, with many mistakes, to say the days of the week in Spanish.

A PROFILE

Heather Sheen

What about your socialization? Can you get into college? How will you function in the real world? These aren't questions that most children hear often, but

I have grown up with them. That's because my younger sister and I were homeschooled all our lives.

Through my parents' dedication, I received a customized, well-rounded education. The flexibility of homeschooling allowed me to move quickly through easy subjects and spend the time necessary to master the harder subjects. I had many social opportunities that would not have been possible were I in a traditional school. My education has taken place in the real world. I feel comfortable socializing with any age group, not just my peers.

Homeschooling has built my confidence to handle all kinds of situations such as running several home businesses, tutoring students in a variety of subjects, giving workshops at conventions, and singing and playing various instruments in front of large groups of people. For example, at age 16, I became one of our church's primary pianist/organists, a position I held for five years. One of my current responsibilities, at age 23, is that I am office manager for my father's management consulting business.

Spiritually, I think that homeschooling has minimized worldly distractions. I can daily spend focused time in God's Word and prayer. My parents set a godly example for me that I strive to follow.

My best friends are my family. We four love to do things together and have attempted everything from singing as a quartet to miniature golfing to lobbying our legislators to touring the British Isles.

Customization, flexibility, family togetherness—I am convinced that homeschooling is the best education any child can have!

■　■　■

There are many reasons why homeschooling is looking better and better to young people in institutional schools. Whatever your reasons for wanting to homeschool, there are several things you should consider doing.

First, read this book. It will give you a lot of substantive background knowledge and insight about homeschooling, the history of institutional schools, and the benefits of home-based education.

An old and very respected set of writings says: "By wisdom a house is built, and through understanding it is established; through knowledge its rooms are filled with rare and beautiful treasures. A wise man has great power, and a man of knowledge increases strength; for waging war you need guidance, and for victory many advisers."[1]

This is not to say that setting off to homeschool will be a battle, but you may run into some resistance. The resistance may come from friends, schoolteachers, school administrators, relatives, neighbors, or parents.

The second thing to do is to remember another important principle in the old and respected set of writings: "Honor your father and your mother, so that you may live long in the land."[2] It is very important to learn about homeschooling and then present your interest in it to your parents in a respectful, humble, and knowledgeable manner. Maybe you could show them this book or a brief, colorful, attractive, and inexpensive booklet like Brian Ray's *Home Schooling on the Threshold: A Survey of Research at the Dawn of the New Millennium*.[3] Do your best to learn and help them understand homeschooling before you get into an adversarial role. If they are positive about it, rejoice.

Third, think about the suggestions in chapter 10, "Learning More or Getting Started in Homeschooling." For example, find a local homeschool support group and attend at least one of their meetings. Meet some families and ask around about who has teenaged homeschool students. Go meet some of them. Talk about homeschooling with them.

Fourth, you will want to think about things like the following:

- What should I do now? How do I continue my education?
- Do I need a diploma?
- Why or why not?
- If I need a diploma, how do I get one?
- What is an apprenticeship and what is its value?
- Do I need a transcript of my studies? If so, how do I create one?
- If I want to go to college or university, how will I get admitted?
- What about friends? How will I have time with them?
- What about sports and extracurricular activities? How do I get involved in them?

There are several books on the market that will give a young person like you important things to think about regarding homeschooling. I cannot endorse everything in all of them because I have not read them all. You could find some of them, however, and carefully consider what they are saying. Discuss the ideas with your parents and friends. One that I fully endorse is *Home Schooling: The Right Choice* by Christopher J. Klicka.[4] I also have confidence in David and Laurie Callihan's book on preparing homeschoolers for college and career[5] and Ted Wade's chapters on homeschooling teenagers.[6] You could look at the materials by Inge Cannon on parents mentoring teens.[7] Other books with which I am less familiar but which are well worth considering are Grace Llewellyn's "liberation" handbook for teenagers[8] and Susannah Sheffer's study of home-schooled adolescent girls and how they develop a sense of self.[9]

If you are the real thoughtful type and want to do some serious reading about the purposes of education and how influential persons and governments often use schools to control and mold people, you might want to consider some more reading. John Taylor Gatto was the public (state) schoolteacher of the year for both New York State and New York City. Then Mr. Gatto wrote *The Underground History of American Education: A Schoolteacher's Intimate Investigation into the Problem of Modern Schooling*.[10] The title mentions America, but it is in many ways about modern "compulsion schooling" in any nation. Gatto writes that after 30 years of teaching in the New York state schools, "an accumulation of disgust and frustration which grew too heavy to be borne finally did me in. . . . I quit."[11] Your eyes may be opened as never before about how government-run institutional schools affect both students and teachers.

If Gatto's book is not enough, take a look at Sheldon Richman's *Separating School and State: How to Liberate America's Families*[12] and Charles Glenn's *The Myth of the Common School*.[13]

A PROFILE

Gary and Beverly Somogie and Their Young Adults

Twenty-one years ago when our first child was born, we had a vision: to be a close-knit family with each member serving the Lord Jesus Christ. The question was how to accomplish this when our worldview collided with that of our society and of the education system? After reading volumes on the subject, we found that home education was the vehicle that could best help us reach our goal. At first, we thought we would only homeschool through the elementary school years, but as our four children grew older, we were encouraged by the fruit of our labor and realized they would continue to benefit from homeschooling right through high school. For this, we received some criticism from family members who thought we were carrying a good thing too far. They were concerned about socialization and whether or not our children would be able to compete in the real world.

We explained that socialization could be either positive or negative and that homeschooling allowed parents, rather than peers, to have more influence in their children's lives. Although some were still skeptical initially, now two of our four children have "graduated" and are successful in their endeavors. Nathan, the oldest, is a sophomore doing well at Gordon College, majoring in business and staying active as a skillful pianist. Sam graduated in 1999 and is a computer technician with a firm in Worcester, Massachusetts. Rachel, a junior in high school, is an accomplished flutist and will participate in the All-Eastern Festival this year. Ruth, a ninth-grader, plays the cello and is on a swim team.

Our critics have come to agree: homeschooling through high school was a good choice.

■ ■ ■

Finally, be sure to realize that homeschooling will not be a bed of roses—an easy endeavor. There are sure to be difficult times and hard work involved. The most difficult thing might be pressure from people who want you to continue in institutional schools. And you may have doubts about whether you are learning all the things you are supposed to learn. You have to wonder who ever dreamed up the list of all those things that every good citizen must know and do. You have to be aware that you are living in a society that has for at least 80 years probably accepted institutional schooling as normal and the best way to learn. Even though there is good evidence that institutional schools are not the best for children and youth, almost everyone acts as if they are.

Be prepared to be different. But also be prepared to experience a new way of life, to feel free, and to be joyful about learning and your future.

Paul Lindstrom, J.D., Ed.D.

In 1967, Brian Barber's parents were dissatisfied with the public school education their son was receiving in Hoffman Estates, Illinois. After discussing the situation with Paul Lindstrom, they decided to remove their son from the state high school to educate him at home. A homeschooling program—Christian Liberty Academy—was born in January 1967.

CLA strongly encouraged parents throughout the U.S. to immediately remove their K-12 children from the state schools and, without local or state approval, to teach them at home using CLA's program of studies. Lindstrom, a public school teacher and 1965 seminary graduate, organized CLA. It promised parents a personally designed curriculum, achievement testing, all books and teaching materials for both student and parents, grading of schoolwork, regular report cards, transcripts, 8th- and 12th-grade graduation diplomas, and legal help if problems ensued.

Most state governments challenged the concept. Christian Liberty Academy homeschooling parents were charged with truancy violations, child abuse, and contributing to the delinquency of minors. Lindstrom traveled from courtroom to courtroom in the 1970s. Working in conjunction with William Ball, Michael Farris, David Gibbs, John Whitehead, and other attorneys, he won significant victories. With each newspaper story and media interview came hordes of additional homeschool students. Judicial decisions and legislative actions made it legal. Book publishers, homeschool providers, magazines catering to home-schooling families, conferences, and book fairs all appeared on the scene.

"What began as a grain of mustard seed in the late 1960s," said Lindstrom in 2001, "has now become an international movement. It's happening everywhere. Recently, I lectured on homeschooling in Russia and Israel. Parents are listening. The future of a nation depends upon the education of its children. Eventually, homeschooling will surpass the number of students in state (public) school education. It is inexpensive! It works! And it is inevitable."

Lindstrom continued to oversee the work of Christian Liberty Academy as its superintendent, write books, and speak at conferences and on radio talk shows until he passed away in 2002. CLA's home-schooling divisions now serve over 50,000 students. Another 900 are being instructed on-campus at the Academy's headquarters located in Arlington Heights, Illinois.

Contact: Christian Liberty Academy, 502 W Euclid Ave., Arlington Heights, IL 60004, tel. 847–259–4444, www.homeschools.org.

■　■　■

CHAPTER 8

Which Approach to Homeschooling?

Homeschooling teaching strategies are approaches to teaching used with home-educated students. Selecting the right strategy for individual students can positively impact the students' learning and retention, thinking skills, motivation to learn, internalization of selected values, and development of constructive character traits. Although selecting homeschooling teaching strategies may appear a complicated and daunting task, it is not difficult in most situations, and tens of thousands of homeschool parents and youth have successfully done it.[1]

It is true that a limited amount of research has been done specifically on homeschooling teaching strategies, but homeschoolers can find research-based guidance from general education research literature and experience-based literature prepared by homeschoolers.

Themes from Relevant Education Research

Before selecting specific teaching strategies, homeschooling parents may benefit from considering four key themes from education research. These concepts generally provide a foundation for effective teaching practices

137

in institutional school settings and many of them are applicable to home-based, parent-led education.

1. TEACHING STRATEGIES THEORY

Researchers and teachers have found that no single teaching approach works in all situations. That is, the effective teaching strategy (or model) depends on the teacher (his personality traits, teaching strengths, and preferences), the student (his interests, learning strengths and limitations, dominant learning style), the content to be taught, and, in homeschooling, the family. A teacher should choose a particular strategy (such as mastery learning, direct instruction, inquiry training), depending on the combination of each of these four factors.

2. TUTORING

Researchers, teachers, and historians generally concur that one-to-one tutoring is, in many ways, the most effective teaching strategy available for most purposes. Tutoring enhances both the tutor's and the student's academic performance and attitude toward subject matter.[2]

3. ACTIVE TEACHING

Teachers can make a difference in students' learning by being proactive and exhibiting particular teaching behaviors. These teaching behaviors generally include (a) choosing appropriate teaching strategies, (b) actively involving students in the learning process, (c) regular and effective monitoring and evaluation of student learning, and (d) careful planning. In a home-based setting, "careful planning" may mean thoughtful planning based on a clear philosophy and goals. It does not necessarily mean, in homeschooling, a tightly structured learning environment that mimics classroom, institutional schooling.

4. DEVELOPMENTALLY APPROPRIATE PRACTICE (DAP)

Individual children are ready to learn and do certain things at certain points in their lives and not before. For many things, there is the right or best timing. In order to ensure that learning can be made meaningful, relevant, and respectful of the child, teachers—including parents—must know and understand (a) child development and learning, (b) age-related human characteristics, (c) the strengths, interests, and needs of each individual child, and (d) the social and cultural contexts in which a child lives.

This list may sound complicated, but it really is not. Much of this knowledge and understanding, in a homeschool setting, comes from the daily time and experience that parents have with their children. Parents also gain this knowledge and related wisdom by talking with other experienced parents and by reading well-grounded books on homeschooling—books such as Michael and Debi Pearl's *To Train Up a Child*[3] and Richard Fugate's *What the Bible Says About Child Training.*[4]

Homeschooling Teaching Strategies

Many studies have shown that home-educated students perform at a higher academic level than the public school average, and research suggests they are doing well in social and emotional development and success in adulthood.[5] Even though few research studies have focused specifically on effective teaching strategies in homeschooling, homeschool parents and youth are clearly doing something right. Much information on teaching strategies for homeschoolers can be found in experienced-based literature written for and by homeschoolers. Listed below, in alphabetical order, are several of the most common teaching strategies or pedagogical approaches that homeschoolers have reported using.[6] Parents regularly mix elements of more than one of these approaches.

1. THE CLASSICAL APPROACH

Teach the tools of learning so they may be used studying any subject. The tools include grammar—mastery of a language; dialectic—logic; and rhetoric—the expressive and creative use of language.

2. LIFESTYLE OF LEARNING OR RELAXED HOMESCHOOLING

Teaching and learning are treated as a seamless and organic part of living within a family, geographical community, local faith community, and nation—that is, the real, everyday world.

3. SCHOOLING AT HOME

Parents generally teach as they were taught in institutional schools. There is a high degree of structure. It often involves active teaching with the teacher having a clear-cut and outstanding role. There is no significant integration of subject areas.

4. STRUCTURED/MASTERY LEARNING

The content to be learned is clearly presented in (usually) consumable booklets or via computers in a sequential, step-by-step manner while emphasizing immediate feedback to the learner. The parent often functions more as a moderator or administrator than as an active teacher.

5. UNIT STUDIES

Unit studies seek to present knowledge in a related way because interrelated concepts are more easily learned and remembered. Subject areas such as math and history are blended together as the teaching is centered around a common theme or project.

6. UNSCHOOLING

This approach emphasizes giving children as much personal freedom to explore and learn about the world as parents can comfortably bear. It does not say that giving them freedom to learn is giving them license to misbehave.[7]

7. WORLDVIEW

This approach emphasizes that all education is value- and belief-driven and that no form of education or schooling can be otherwise. It purposely and explicitly integrates a particular worldview in curriculum materials, activities, and ways of thinking. An example is the Principle Approach, which focuses on researching a religious writing to identify basic principles or truths, reasoning from these truths through an academic subject such as history or politics, relating the principles to the student's own character and self-government, and recording in writing the application of the principles and ideas to life and living.

These homeschooling approaches involve many elements of effective teaching strategies promoted by educational researchers and theoreticians. Homeschoolers' use of these approaches and emphasis on academics[8] appear to be working well. Keys to the students' success appear to involve the following interdependent features:[9] (a) making learning at home "an interactive process rather than a series of tasks to be tackled," allowing for rich student-teacher conversation, individualization, taking advantage of teachable moments, and ensuring mastery before moving forward;[10] (b) tutoring (concentrated time on task, individualization); (c) social capital and value communities; (d) increased academic engaged time; (e) positive, multiage social interactions; and (f) high parental involvement.

A PROFILE

Roberta Sue Welch

Pat and Sue Welch published, for many years, *The Teaching Home*, a Christian magazine for home educators. *The Teaching Home* started as a one-page newsletter in 1980. In 1983 it became a national newsletter and initiated a program to work with and help state organizations. *The Teaching Home* grew to be 64-page, bimonthly magazine with a circulation of 100,000 worldwide in 2001.

The purpose of *The Teaching Home* is to provide information, inspiration, and support to Christian homeschool families publishing articles, letters, and teaching tips written mostly by homeschoolers themselves, all from a distinctively Christian perspective.

The Teaching Home sells back issues and furnishes support services to Christian homeschool state organizations.

The Welch family has homeschooled all three of their children throughout their entire education, continuing now in college-level studies at home. Mrs. Welch remarks, "Beside the benefits of academics, character, and spiritual values, I believe that homeschooling is one of the nicest things that you can do for your child. We have enjoyed learning, traveling, and living life together with our children. They have been nurtured and protected by adults that love them."

Contact: The Teaching Home, P. O. Box 20219, Portland, OR 97294, tel. 503–253–9633, tth@TeachingHome.com, www.TeachingHome.com.

■ ■ ■

Choosing Homeschooling Teaching Strategies

Many parents grow into using a teaching strategy or strategies. They are open to modifying their strategy as they, their individual children, and their family change over the years. Parents should consider these guidelines as they try to identify the strategy most likely to work well for them:

- Reflecting upon and articulating a personal philosophy of education. They can do this by (a) reading literature on the philosophy of education, homeschooling, and their personal worldview; (b) talking with close friends and family members about education; (c) considering their own educational experiences; and (d) writing down their key educational beliefs and goals.
- Joining a local homeschool support group that supports their philosophy of education and includes experienced homeschoolers.
- Subscribing to a local homeschool newsletter and at least two homeschool magazines that support their basic philosophy to learn how other families practice home-based education.
- Examining their personal preferences, strengths, weaknesses, and interests with respect to their complementary roles as parent, heads of families, communicator, teacher, and learner.
- Thinking about their children individually and as a group with respect to their personal

preferences, strengths, weaknesses, and interests as communicators, children, learners, and students of subject matter.

- Seeking outside help if they have children with an unusual need such as a learning disability, giftedness, or a special interest. Sources of help might include National Challenged Homeschoolers Associated Network (see Appendix), local private consultants, veteran homeschoolers, and mentors.

Parents should then move ahead with confidence in their best judgment. They know their children best and care about them more than does anyone else. As they teach and guide their children, parents will have ample opportunity and time to observe and evaluate their children's learning, attitudes, and progress—academic, social, emotional, and spiritual. They have been doing this since the birth of their child and can continue doing so. Teaching strategies can be modified based on what seems to work best for their individual families.

A PROFILE

Cathy Duffy

Cathy Duffy is motivated by individualizing every child's education, freely chosen high standards, and a good education for all students. She is considered one of America's leading home education curriculum reviewers and is the author of the two-volume *Christian*

Home Educators' Curriculum Manual (elementary grades and junior/senior high).

The impetus for exploring the array of curriculum grew from Cathy's experience home educating her own three sons. Cathy and her husband Michael began homeschooling in 1982, graduating their youngest in 1997. While their youngest son, Matthew, is still in college, their two older sons, Christopher and Joshua, have gone on through college into successful careers in graphic design and computer systems, respectively.

Cathy's educational research and experience convinced her of the value of individualizing education to achieve the best results for each child. She was one of the first to sound the alarm regarding government efforts to standardize goals, outcomes, and methodology for all students. The results of her research were published in her book *Government Nannies: The Cradle-to-Grave Agenda of Goals 2000 and Outcome-Based Education.*

In 1998, as part of a positive attack on education woes in inner cities, Cathy helped establish the Children's Scholarship Fund in Los Angeles, a private scholarship program designed to enable low-income children to attend private K-12 schools.

The combination of these experiences resulted in Cathy's current vision of using computer technology to create outstanding, yet affordable, educational models that challenge the national standards. She envisions the creation of an internet-based education provider offering modular courses based on classical methodology combined with a Christian worldview that can be accessed by students anywhere in the world.

Contact Cathy Duffy and ask about her books at Grove Publishing, 16172 Huxley Circle, Westminster, CA 92683, tel. 714–841–1220, www.grovepublishing.com.

■ ■ ■

CHAPTER 9

Odds and Ends—More Common Questions

Even after reading research reports on how well homeschool students do, how many families through homeschooling have found the close family relationships they have always wanted, and hearing great philosophical arguments supporting home-schooling, many parents still have a lot of questions and doubts. Here are a few of them, with answers.

Am I Qualified?

Perhaps you are thinking, "I have only a high school education myself. I hate math. I do not know a foreign language. I do not know much science." One of your most important qualifications, as a parent, is that you care—a lot—about your children. You love them more than does anyone else. Much more than do licensed teachers and administrators in institutional schools. Second, you are willing either to learn something so that you can teach it to your children or to find someone or some educational resource that can teach what you are not prepared or willing to teach. You are not afraid of a little hard work. This may sound too simple, but it is true.

Thousands upon thousands of parents have found that their own willingness to learn or to be resourceful in helping their children learn is the key to their children's success. To the joyful surprise of the parents, this willingness to learn also leads to the parents themselves learning more than they ever dreamed possible. In addition, the research of this author and many scholars repeatedly shows that both the children of homeschool parents with doctorates and the children of homeschool parents who did not even earn a high school (secondary) diploma are doing very well academically.

For a little more encouragement in this area, you might want to look at Terry Dorian and Zan Tyler's book *Anyone Can Homeschool*.[1] And see other chapters of this book to study the research on how homeschool children and families do in many areas of life.

A PROFILE

Zan Tyler

Zan Tyler, coauthor of the book *Anyone Can Homeschool*, has devoted the last 17 years of her life to efforts that make homeschooling accessible to everyone who wants to homeschool.

Tyler is one of the true pioneers of the modern-day home education movement. When she and her husband began homeschooling in 1984, she was threatened with jail. Since then she has worked tirelessly through writing, speaking, and legislative efforts to promote a positive climate for homeschooling, both in her native South Carolina and nationally. In the early

1990s, she spearheaded groundbreaking legislative work culminating in the establishment of the private South Carolina Association of Independent Home Schools (SCAIHS) as an approval agency for homeschooling families on a par equal with local school boards. In addition to being its founder, Tyler served as president of SCAIHS for 10 years.

In February 2000, Tyler left SCAIHS to become executive editor of the Home-Based Education Channel for Christianity.com. This new endeavor gives her an international platform for promoting home education and supporting homeschooling families.

Tyler's main mission has been to encourage and empower parents to take charge of their children's education. In addition, she has strived to inspire, educate, support, and equip parents in the task of homeschooling. She believes that homeschooling is a vital tool for spiritual, moral, family, and educational revival, and this belief has been the driving force behind her work.

The Tylers' sons, who were homeschooled from kindergarten through high school, are attending college on a variety of athletic, leadership, and academic scholarships. Joe and Zan continue to homeschool their daughter.

For further information or to have Mrs. Tyler speak to your group or state convention, contact her at ztyler@crosswalk.com, www.crosswalk.com (Home-Based Education Channel), www.scaihs.org, tel. 803–788–6814.

■ ■ ■

What About Sports?

Almost every small town or large city has sports or athletic leagues. Some of these are crawling with soccer, football, and baseball leagues, boys and girls clubs, the YMCA, the YWCA, hiking clubs, shooting teams, and the list goes on. Children and youth do not have to attend public or private schools in order to find sports teams to which they can belong. And a young person need not be on a team in a league to participate in sports. Many children and youth throughout history, including today, just go down to the local park or recreation center two or three times per week to play intensive, or low-key, sports with whomever is there.

Sometimes it is harder to find organized sports as youth get into their teen years if they are not attending institutional schools. But there are several possibilities. First, ask a private (independent) school if he or she may participate; their rules and policies are often more flexible than those of public/state schools.

Second, sometimes the law requires public/state school sports programs to give access to homeschool students. It must be remembered, however, that often students must come under significant government control in order to participate in government-related or government-controlled sports programs.

Third, the issue of access to and participation in organized sports offers a prime opportunity for parents and youth to consider and discuss whether such participation is as important as some societies make it out to be. What is more important, developing self-disciplined habits that lead to a life of wholesome physical health or merely playing varsity sports in secondary or high school, then becoming physically unfit and a watcher of televised sports for the rest of your life?

What Extracurricular Activities Are Available to Homeschoolers?

Many sports activities in local communities were just listed above. Many additional activities and groups available to homeschoolers are not necessarily linked to institutional schools. These include music clubs, instrumental bands, book reading clubs, Boy Scouts, Girl Scouts, scoutlike programs operated by churches such as AWANA and Pioneer Club, wood-carving clubs, computer clubs, 4-H, shooting clubs, Future Farmers of America, Bible quizzing, Keepers of the Faith, Keepers at Home, folk dance clubs, model railroad organizations, remote-controlled airplane clubs, book reading/discussion groups, poetry clubs, dance classes, music classes, foreign language clubs, and a multitude of other associations. Almost any homeschool newsletter or support group or organization will quickly point the interested parent or youth to a host of these opportunities. In addition, many home educators start an interest group if the one they want does not exist.

What Field Trips Are Available to Homeschoolers?

The possibilities are endless. Homeschoolers have probably come up with more creative and out-of-the-way field trip explorations than most institutional schoolteachers have ever imagined—often because homeschool groups' schedules are very flexible and because homeschoolers can often bring smaller groups of children and more adult supervisors than can the school class.

Here are some examples: art museum, zoo (zoological garden), potato chip factory, fish processing plant, glass blowing studio, pottery studio, museum of science and industry, newspaper publishing company, television station, radio station, government capitol building, legislative/assembly/parliament offices, historic buildings, water sewage treatment plant, plant nursery, beef production ranch, farm, computer software company, shoemaker shop, candlemaker shop, butcher shop, florist shop, deep-sea fishing vessel, military base, military naval ship, and airport.

What About Socialization?

Do they have any friends? Children who are home-schooled enjoy talking to their friends, their friends' parents, old people in the lines (queues) in grocery stores, and the auto mechanic. One day my veterinarian called me to talk about my sheep's problems. Once the veterinarian found out what the National Home Education Research Institute does, he volunteered, "Do you know what I notice about homeschool kids?" I asked, "What?" "When they come into my office with their parents, they talk with me." Upon a little further probing, I found out that most other children and youth who come into his office avoid conversing with him or are not very agile at discussing things with him; they are not accustomed to conversing with a variety of adults.

Unless parents isolate themselves from contact with other humans and forbid their children from contact with other humans, then the opportunity for social interaction is grand for homeschoolers. People are social by nature, and the vast majority of homeschoolers engage in a wide variety of activities with persons of all ages. In fact, homeschool children and youth find it very normal to—and are very comfortable with—talk and play and learn with persons of all ages. They are not confined to six hours per day, five days per week, 185 days per year, for 13 or more years, largely with same-age peers.

The research described earlier in this book supports the notion that homeschool youth are healthy—socially, psychologically, and emotionally. Normal life for homeschoolers is interacting with whomever comes along related to whatever purpose the student or family has in mind. Being segregated by age does not dictate a homeschooler's life. Goals and vision and educational objectives determine with whom, and with what ages of people, he or she will be each day. Their friends are older, younger, the same age, from down the street, from across town, from the local synagogue or church, from the nearby public/state school, or from the private scout club. Most people live most of their lives this way once they finish school.

In fact, when asked about the real world, most homeschoolers chuckle and respond that life in the four walls of a school is far from the real world and that they have always been living in the real world.

Can Someone Else Homeschool My Children?

Homeschooling, by definition, is family-based, home-based, and usually parent-led—with parents in charge of the child's education. If a parent wants another parent to do all the teaching and be in charge of the child, then it is probably not homeschooling. Maybe it is a small private school or a dame school. There are, however, many ways in which parents do not do all the teaching of their own children.

This is a key point. In homeschooling, parents recognize their own responsibility and right to direct the education and upbringing of their child. As both discussed and alluded to earlier, however, parents and children may choose from many learning opportunities, classes, field trips, and so forth to be a part of the children's education. Often classes for a specific subject are taught by someone other than the child's parent. Someone else may teach science, advanced mathematics, computer programming, Latin, or piano. This is a common, legitimate, and philosophically agreeable practice in the context of homeschooling. It is also common for a group of families to develop more elaborate systems of helping one another homeschool. For example, some families use cooperatives (see below).

What About Co-ops (Cooperatives)?

Homeschoolers have been creating cooperatives (co-ops) throughout the more than two decades of the modern homeschool movement. In a co-op, a number of parents volunteer and share their teaching expertise or skill in teaching one another's children. For example, families may form a co-op. All meet two mornings per week for three hours at each meeting. One mother teaches biology, one father teaches wood-carving, and another mother teaches a foreign language during these times. The other parents act as teaching aides, keep students engaged in the learning activities, and care for small children. After the classes, the families eat lunch together and the children play awhile before they all return home. This works in varied ways, limited only by the creativity and abilities of the participants.

What Is the Daily Routine?

The daily routine is whatever you choose. You would do well to talk with several homeschool parents about how they structure their days. They will give you many practical ideas about what to try. You will soon realize that homeschooling involves no magic formula but a lot of flexibility and choice. Many parents start homeschooling by trying to imitate all the things they experienced in institutional schools, but they quickly realize how absurd and unnecessary this is in the home setting.

Most families do the more formal or concentrated academic studies (e.g., math content, grammar study, systematic foreign language) in the morning or early afternoon. Afternoons tend to be more flexible. Each family gets to develop its own unique style.

How should this be done? That depends on factors such as:

- The curriculum approach the parents (or youth) decide to use (see discussion in previous chapter).
- The teaching strategy the parents decide to use (see discussion in previous chapter).
- The schedules of any parents who work outside the home.
- Whether the parent and children are most mentally alert very early in the morning or a bit later.
- Whether a set quantity of curriculum content is to be learned over the course of 7 months, 9 months, or 12 months.
- Whether the family chooses a daily and yearly schedule that is more structured, carefully planned, and independent of season or one that is more flexible or seasonable. A flexible schedule is more accepting of serendipity, but a seasonal schedule is sometimes necessary, as for farm families, for example.
- The amount of experience with homeschooling.

Over the months and years, most homeschool families mature and change their schedules and routines as well as their teaching and learning habits. They refine their philosophies as their children grow older and as new ideas spring forth. This is natural and helpful.

What Curriculum Should I Use?

If a person new to homeschooling meets a veteran who says there is one best way and one best curriculum for all homeschoolers, the new person should quickly depart from the presence of that veteran. I hope I have made it clear that there is no one best system for all homeschoolers to follow. Homeschooling lets parents carefully and wisely evaluate curriculum materials and instructional approaches. In choosing materials and strategies, parents should consider their own educational philosophy and talents, their child's special gifts and unique needs, as well as their family's unique character.

This is not to say, however, that the choices need to be complicated, anxiety producing, or ponderous. The new homeschooler should talk with a variety of home-schoolers who share similar values and beliefs, look at a variety of curriculum materials, then confidently choose some things with which to begin. New home-school parents should spend cautiously at first to avoid wasting money on materials they later find unsatisfactory for their family. Yet education does cost money, and parents are educating themselves about what is good curriculum for their families. In the United States, parents spend, on average, $300 to $600 per year per child for home education materials. They should not be afraid of spending money, and they should anticipate that they will make some wrong choices once in a while. (See chapter 10, "Lerning More or Getting Started."

Are All Curriculum Materials Religous?

You may have noticed that many religious people homeschool. You may be asking yourself whether all the curriculum materials, Christian or otherwise, are religious. Of course, everyone is, in a sense, religious. This is true in that every person has a set of beliefs that informs his or her behavior and ways of dealing with the world and God, regardless of whether he or she believes in a supernatural power. Yet some people are more aware than others of their own religious ideas; some are more confident about them; some are more vocal about them; and some are more aware that religious ideas saturate all educational materials and institutions. That being said, it is true that most homeschoolers these days are confidently religious. At this historical moment, most homeschoolers are Christians. However, not all are.

Many homeschoolers do not focus on religious ideas or reasons for homeschooling, and many curriculum materials do not focus on religious themes or coherent religious belief systems. Many textbooks, films, movies, computer software programs, online Internet-based courses, workbooks, books, science kits, and other materials appear religiously neutral. Homeschooling has grown so much around the world that of curriculum producers have developed so many products that almost anyone of any religious—or supposedly nonreligious—persuasion can find plenty of materials to purchase or use.

A FIRST-PERSON PROFILE

Pat Montgomery, Ed.D.

Becoming a teacher was not exactly a choice for me; it was more of a life assignment. I was a nun in the religious Congregation of Divine Providence, and since that was, primarily, a teaching order of nuns, I was assigned to teach. That was back in 1953.

Fourteen years later, after leaving religious life, earning a Bachelor of Education from Duquesne University in Pittsburgh, Pennsylvania, earning a Master of Arts in child development from the University of Michigan at Ann Arbor, marrying Jim Montgomery, and giving birth to two children, I started Clonlara School.

A few years after founding Clonlara, I earned a Ph.D. in educational leadership and alternative education from Wayne State University in Detroit.

In 1977, two families asked me to put the resources of Clonlara, a private school, behind them while they taught their own children at home. That seemed the most logical thing in the world to me. Teach your own so as to avoid the expense and time commitment of founding a school. Teach your own so that your own philosophy and practice will be the order of each day. It was my chance to share with other parents the things I had learned over the years in conventional schools and in the alternative setting of Clonlara. Thus began Clonlara School Home Based Education Program (CSHBEP).

The campus school currently enrolls 62 students, ages 5 through 18. The CSHBEP enrolls 7,500 students who reside in each of the 50 United States and in 25 other countries.

■ ■ ■

What About Computers and Science Equipment?

Homeschool students probably have more personal access to computers and the Internet than do the public/state school students. About five years ago, I found that about 85 percent of homeschool families in the United States owned a computer, while the national average was only about 34 percent.[2] More recent research confirms that computer usage is very high among homeschoolers.[3] Used, adequate computers are within the financial reach of most families who are reading this book. At the same time, however, most people should realize that a computer is not a necessary element of an excellent education. A young person or adult who is well-educated in the three R's can learn to use a computer for the basics of word processing, spreadsheets, databases, and Internet travel in a relatively short time.

The quality and quantity of science curricula and science equipment in state-run schools is highly variable. Even where it is available and of high quality, many elementary school students spend little time studying science and using science equipment, and their teachers have little more special training in science than the common parent does. In secondary schools, the percentage of students who study science and use expensive equipment is also highly variable.

On the other hand, homeschoolers have the opportunity to spend large amounts of time studying science if they so choose. If a particular young or older student has a special interest or gifting in science, he or she may be encouraged to delve deeply and for long periods of time into the scientific pursuit. Furthermore, advanced and expensive equipment is not necessary to a sound basic science education.

Most science process skills and ways of thinking can be taught very well with ordinary household materials, equipment, liquids, and solvents. Several excellent science curricula and programs have been developed for use by homeschoolers. Many of these use very inexpensive materials and items easily found around the home, in hardware stores, and in pharmacies. If families want more expensive equipment like a high-quality microscope, they can purchase it alone or share the cost with another family or two.[4]

Parents of a student needing the help of teachers more knowledgeable or capable in science than they should consider these alternatives:

- Join with other families in forming a science cooperative or class taught by a science specialist or scientist who has teaching skill.
- Arrange for the young person to have a science mentor (or apprenticeship).
- Enroll your child in a correspondence program or a science class at a local private secondary school or university.

Is It Legal?

What is the law? Laws vary from nation to nation and state to state (or county, canton, province). In the United States, for example, homeschooling is legal in every one or the 50 states and every territory. In Alaska, if parents never send away their children to be under the authority and control of the state school, then they do not have to have any contact with the state about the education of their children. In Massachusetts, on the other hand, a state school committee may examine the competency of the parents to teach their children but may not require teacher certification or advanced or college degrees. As an example of another nation, in Germany the state strictly controls education, and homeschooling is still basically treated as illegal.

The best way to get an initial understanding of the law regarding homeschooling is to contact home-school organizations. An excellent one that works extensively in the United States and with home-schoolers in many other nations is the Home School Legal Defense Association (listed in the Appendix). Parents should also contact their own state/province/canton private homeschool organization for information. They might also learn some important things by contacting government agencies about the law, but I believe they should do this only after getting advice from homeschool-friendly organizations, possibly making only anonymous contact with government agencies.

What Should I Do If English Is Not My First Language?

Many parents in this situation homeschool their children. Even if a parent's first language is not the common language of his or her community or nation, there are many ways to successfully homeschool the children.

The concern, of course, is usually that the children will not learn the common language if it is not the parents' first language and therefore will be at some disadvantage growing up. There are several things to consider in this regard.

First, it is a blessing to a child (who will later be an adult) to learn more than one language. Millions of parents (especially in America) wish their children had the advantage of speaking two languages.

Second, while making sure that their home-schooled children learn the common language, the parents themselves will be especially motivated to learn the common language, more so than if they sent their children away to be taught by others in schools.

Third, there are several ways to ensure that the children in this type of family do learn well the common language.

To begin, a homeschool family in which the parents do not speak English (or the common language) should do the same basic things that other homeschool families do in their communities (see chapter 10, "Learning More or Getting Started in Homeschooling"). For example, they should join and participate in a local support group, attend homeschool conferences, and subscribe to some homeschool magazines.

Second, the family can purchase some curriculum materials in English and some in the language of the parents. The non-English-speaking parent can focus on teaching some subjects while having others teach their children in other subjects, perhaps using cooperatives, tutors, or videotapes. The parents should be sure to engage their children in church and community activities that will help them learn the common language, while learning other content and serving other people.

Finally, the parents should be sure to be learning the common language themselves in order to serve as a good role model for their children and to become active and serving members of their communities and churches.

A PROFILE FROM CANADA

Dan and Deanna Woodard in Canada

Dan and Deanna Woodard are homeschool parents of their three boys, Joseph (14), Jacob (11), and Jonathan (9). They have been homeschooling for nine years and live in Alberta, Canada.

Dan and Deanna are missionaries with InterAct Ministries. For 20 years they have assisted Native Indian leadership in developing disciples, leaders, and churches in northwestern Ontario and Manitoba. Dan presently serves as the Inter-Mission Cooperative Outreach Administrator and Native Church Consultant. This opportunity has led Dan and Deanna to be more involved in equipping new missionaries in 10 mission agencies across Canada, as well as developing Native Indian leadership for Native churches.

In recent years Dan has assisted Native leadership in Winnipeg in developing a three-year Bible curriculum on Native Identity. Research shows that traditionally Native parents and grandparents assumed total responsibility in the educating of their children. Five generations of Canada's residential schools brought a crushing loss to this tradition.

Today Canadian Native people are experiencing a rebirth of their traditions and culture. Dan believes this resurgence of Native identity is a move of God. He considers this a return to the Hebraic model of culture in contrast to the Greek institutional model of mainstream contemporary society.

Dan and Deanna have assisted several Native parents in starting schooling at home. "This has stimulated our vision for the homeschool movement to catch on with Native parents all across Canada," Dan reflects. "It is the most natural way for parents to pass their values, culture, heritage, and Christian faith to the next generation."

Dan served as secretary of the Manitoba Association of Christian Home Schools (www.machs.ca) from 1995 to 1999. Deanna served during this time as exhibitor coordinator of the annual homeschool conference in Winnipeg.

Contact: Dan and Deanna Woodard, InterAct Ministries, P. O. Box 863, Carstairs, Alberta T0M 0N0, Canada, tel. 403–337–4899, fax 403–265–7737, DanandDeanna@compuserve.com, www.interactministries.org.

■ ■ ■

How Do We Take Our Children Out of State/Public Schools?

If your children are already in public/state schools and you want to take them out, begin by contacting your state/province/canton private homeschool organization for information. Start your search for information with individuals and organizations you know to be friendly toward parental rights and homeschooling. Second, I strongly suggest that you or a member of your family become a member of the Home School Legal Defense Association (HSLDA) in the U.S., HSLDA of Canada, or a similar organization in your own country before removing your children from a state school. Seek the advice of veteran homeschool leaders and of organizations like HSLDA.

You should prepare yourself, then act prudently. Some state school officials are friendly but others are hostile to homeschooling. In all of this, however, parents should remember and be confident in the fact that God has given them the fundamental and unalienable right to direct the education and upbringing of their children.

CHAPTER 10

Learning More or Getting Started in Homeschooling

You have taken a notable step by reading this book. I will try, in this chapter, to point you toward some of the most important services and information that will get you off to a quick, efficient, and rewarding beginning to homeschooling.

Here are the most pertinent subjects to consider:

- How to find personal support in your local community, state, province, county, or nation
- What printed literature to read at the beginning of your adventure into home education
- How to make decisions about which curriculum to use and how to teach your children
- Legal and research services
- The importance of a philosophy of education

All of these topics are of immediate interest and importance to anyone relatively new to home education. At the same time, however, you have already addressed many of these issues if you are already a parent. This is true because every parent is *already* the most important educator of his or her own children.

Personal Support

You need to find, meet, and get to know people in your city or locale who are experienced homeschoolers. Find homeschool groups in telephone directories, at church, and on the Internet. Ask around—find them by word of mouth. They will likely be your first valuable help and resource once you have made the decision to home educate your children.

Statewide/Provincial/Canton/National Organizations

Statewide/provincial/canton/national private organizations are typically very good at understanding the laws and regulations of the state that pertain to home education. Many of them sponsor homeschool conferences and curriculum fairs. They lobby lawmakers and keep an eye on changes in the law that may affect the ability of families to engage freely in home education. They often publish newsletters. Stay in contact with them; subscribe to the newsletter; support your local, regional, and national homeschool organizations in any way you can.

Large homeschool organizations will help you find support groups in your city or town. See the Appendix of this book to help you find the homeschool organization in your state (region, nation). Contact them and ask how to order whatever would be helpful for finding out about home education in your area, and ask them how to find a local support group in your city.

Dallas K. Miller, Q.C. in Canada

Dallas K. Miller has been a lawyer since 1985 and, in addition to his law degree (LL.B.), holds a B.A. (history) and a Bachelor of Religious Education degree (B.R.E). He was appointed Queen's Counsel in 1998. In his legal practice, Dallas has handled cases before the Supreme Court of Canada. He has also been active in litigation and lobbying on pro-life, pro-family, and religious freedom issues throughout his career. He is the senior counsel and executive director of the Home School Legal Defence Association of Canada (HSLDA), a membership organization that provides legal assistance to families that homeschool their children. HSLDA is the only national home education organization in Canada and serves the homeschool community by providing legal advocacy on behalf of families.

Dallas and his wife, Marjorie, were introduced to homeschooling through their friend and pastor, Dan Reinhardt, in 1994. Dallas has always been interested in constitutional aspects of family autonomy and parental rights, but only after he was introduced to homeschooling did his vision to defend parental rights take on an entirely new meaning. Marjorie and Dallas homeschool their two teens, Sean (18) and Chelsea (15). They see homeschooling as God's plan to pass on to their children a solid Christian worldview and an opportunity to build godly character into their lives.

As senior counsel and executive director of HSLDA, Dallas has had the privilege of speaking to thousands of parents across Canada. In addition to speaking in every one of the 10 Canadian provinces on homeschooling, Dallas has represented HSLDA at the World Congress on the Family II in Geneva (1999) and at the United Nations Workers Training Conference sponsored by Focus on the Family Canada in New York (2000).

In addition to working hard to expand parental liberty and family autonomy and ensuring that parents have the right to continue to homeschool, one of Dallas's goals is to see fathers across Canada return to their biblical role and involve themselves fully in the homeschooling process. Dallas is convinced that homeschooling helps strengthen the family and that stronger families will raise stronger future generations that will make for a stronger nation. Dallas sees HSLDA and the homeschool movement as playing a key role in strengthening Canada's future and acting as a godly fortress against the rising tide of secularism and moral decay.

"As we enter the new millennium," Dallas says, "the new education methodology of homeschooling will expand and challenge Canadian culture." Dallas Miller and HSLDA of Canada are pleased to be at the forefront of such an exciting movement.

Contact: Home School Legal Defence Association of Canada, #2–3295 Dunmore Rd. SE, Medicine Hat, Alberta T1B 3R2, tel. 403–528–2704, info@hsldacanada.org, www.hsldacanada.org.

Local Support Groups

Most cities and even some small towns in the U.S. and Canada have local home education support groups. They are becoming more common in other nations. These groups come in many varieties. Their basic purpose, however, is usually to support and encourage individual homeschooling families in whatever way they can. Some of the things that they do are publish newsletters, hold monthly meetings, sponsor science fairs and used-curriculum exchanges, plan field trips, and network home educators so that they can learn from and encourage one another.

Ask your statewide, provincial, or nationwide organization to put you in contact with the local support group in your city or town. You could also ask friends who homeschool about the different support groups in your city. Go to the meetings and meet people. Subscribe to the local newsletter. Find out what written materials they suggest will help you. Spend a little money and read. Others will help you, but you must put some significant energy into learning on your own.

Talk with experienced home educators in your locality and find out what they do or have done with respect to curriculum materials and pedagogy—how do they teach? Ask them about the strengths and weaknesses of various methods, learning approaches, and curriculum materials. Remember that each person is giving you a personal and family story. If anyone tells you that method X or curriculum Y is *the only* way to go, be particularly cautious and wary of his or her general advice.

Please remember that the vast majority of people who serve in local, statewide, provincial, or regional homeschool organizations are volunteers. They strongly believe in home education, and they want to serve you the best way they can. But they are volunteers and have families and other responsibilities besides the homeschool group. Please do not expect other experienced homeschoolers to have tremendous amounts of time to spend with you. They are busy being mothers, fathers, home educators, businessmen, craftsmen, and church members. Respect their volunteerism, be patient while you wait for them to respond to you, and try to encourage them in any way you can.

Resources

Get ready to learn! Even if you did not particularly like school as a youngster, you will probably get very excited about learning as you get involved in home educating your children. Besides finding and learning from other experienced homeschoolers, you need to read, read, and read some more.

BOOKS

There are many books that can get you off to a great start. For example, I think highly of *The Right Choice: Home Schooling*,[1] by attorney and speaker Christopher Klicka, and of *The Christian Home*

School,[2] by author and speaker Gregg Harris. My own book *Home Schooling on the Threshold: A Survey of Research at the Dawn of the New Millennium* is a comprehensive, full-color report on many aspects of homeschooling including academic achievement, socialization, population growth, success in adulthood; it is available from the National Home Education Research Institute (NHERI) listed in the Appendix.[3] Besides general books on home education, parents need to give special attention to child training if they want the whole enterprise to be successful. In this area, I recommend *To Train Up a Child* by Michael and Debi Pearl and Richard Fugate's book on child training.[4] I also recommend a book that every husband should read—*The Homeschooling Father*,[5] by Michael Farris, attorney, speaker, and homeschool father of 10 children.

RADIO PROGRAMS

To learn about the radio program *Home School Heartbeat*, contact the Home School Legal Defense Association, which is listed in the Appendix.[6] You might also want to listen to *Homeschooling USA*.[7]

MAGAZINES

Several excellent magazines with long and successful track records are published. Ask other homeschoolers about them.

The Internet

The world of information about homeschooling and parent-led instruction, distance learning courses, and online education is growing extremely rapidly on the World Wide Web, so fast that it is impossible for anyone to list the addresses of all the worthy Web sites, resources, and so forth. Although use of computers and the Internet are not essential to a solid academic education, parents and their children can wisely use them as part of a good education. The possibilities are myriad.

It is fairly simple to enter the world of home-schooling and educational courses online. One can begin at the sites of historically dependable and trusted individuals, businesses, and organizations and branch out from there. Three sites that I recommend are National Home Education Research Institute (www.nheri.org), The Teaching Home (www.teaching-home.com), and the Home School Legal Defense Association (www.hslda.org). (See the Appendix for more sites.) These will lead the inquisitive to many other good and useful sites in the quest to become better educated homeschoolers and to provide an excellent education for one's children.

Curriculum

What and how to teach are often near the top of the list of new home educators' concerns. Curriculum and teaching approaches, however, are relatively complicated and detailed topics. In this arena, your local support group friends, reading on your own, attending conferences, developing your philosophy over time, and so forth are essential to success.

What and how you teach will most likely develop and improve over time. Research, and my experience, tell me that most home educators change the *what* and *how* of their curriculum several times over the course of years. Be prepared for successes—and sometimes disappointments. Remember, however, that you may always make changes and that changes do not necessarily mean your children are falling behind. (See also chapter 8, "Which Approach to Homeschooling?)

CURRICULUM FAIRS

Attend some curriculum fairs or conferences. Go with wisdom and discretion. Give yourself time to observe, read, and discuss the materials. Do not be too quick to spend your money at these fairs. Plan ahead, if you can, by talking with people to determine what you would like to examine and review at the fair. Go with a seasoned homeschooler you respect who can help you clarify what you need to purchase.

BOOKS ON CURRICULA

Many homeschool authors write about and review curriculum materials. Recognize that they have their own viewpoints and families that may be different from yours. However, reading their books can be an efficient way to familiarize yourself with the abundance of curricula available to home educators. You can browse through one of these manuals that reviews all, or at least most, of the programs and publishers. Cathy Duffy[8] and Mary Pride publish such books.[9]

Philosophy of Teaching

There are many approaches to homeschooling pedagogy. Some of the books and magazines that I have already mentioned will help you determine what you should do. Be prayerful, and again remember to be cautious about those who tell you or imply that there is only one right way. (See also chapter 8, "Which Approach to Homeschooling?")

As a final thought on curriculum, you may wonder about the cost of purchasing curriculum materials for your children. How much money home educators spend varies widely. You may spend as little as $50 per child per year. You may spend as much as $1,000 per child. Research that I have done indicates that $400 to $600 per child per year is very common in the U.S.

Legal Services

The Home School Legal Defense Association (HSLDA; listed in the Appendix) is an excellent organization with a long and successful service record. It is a Christian organization but serves people regardless of their religious beliefs. You should probably become a member of HSLDA if you live in the United States. There is an HSLDA of Canada, also. A similar organization was recently founded in Germany. If you live in a country without such an organization, you should contact HSLDA of the U.S. and ask about joining them. Even if you never need their legal services, you are helping people all over the United States and in other countries who do need legal assistance. In addition, your state's or nation's laws could change and become less friendly to home education.

A PROFILE

Christopher J. Klicka, J.D.

Christopher J. Klicka has served as senior counsel for the Home School Legal Defense Association since 1985. After writing a 350-page analysis of the compulsory attendance laws and cases pertaining to homeschooling, he began as the first full-time lawyer for HSLDA defending the right of parents to choose homeschooling, even though he and his wife, Tracy, did not have any children at the time.

Chris began testifying in state legislatures, working on homeschool legislation, and representing families in court. He argued before five state supreme courts, worked on federal civil rights cases, and handled many trials and administrative hearings and appeals. Chris has handled approximately 6,000 legal conflicts on behalf of homeschool parents who were being threatened or harassed by states' local school districts. Chris has testified before Congress and has led many of the lobbying efforts on Capitol Hill. He played a major role leading the lobbying efforts to stop national testing, preventing the ratification of the United Nations Convention on the Rights of the Child, and repealing the most significant parts of Goals 2000.

Chris has spoken before hundreds of state home-school conventions and has traveled abroad, helping to legalize homeschooling in South Africa and Canada. He has worked to help homeschoolers in Japan, Germany, South Africa, and Canada to start legal defense associations for homeschoolers.

Chris's goal is to help guard and win the right of parents throughout the United States and many other nations to homeschool their children with minimal regulation. He believes that the right to homeschool opens the door to the gospel of Jesus Christ and for discipling children in the Word of God. As long as the homeschool movement puts Jesus Christ first, it will continue to win the court battles and legislative efforts.

Chris and Tracy homeschool their seven children, and he has dedicated his life to defending home-schoolers before the legislatures, Congress, and the courts. When Chris started working at Home School Legal Defense Association, homeschooling was legal in only five states. Now it is legal in all 50 states. Chris has worked with many homeschool organizations and the growing team of attorneys and personnel with Home School Legal Defense Association to help bring this about. But ultimately, Chris wants to give all the glory to God since God has been merciful and graciously given homeschool families the protection they need to train their children in the Lord.

Families can join the Home School Legal Defense Association for $100 per year. HSLDA agrees to defend any member family in court and helps home-schoolers if universities or the military discriminate against them as they try to enroll or enlist. HSLDA works in state legislatures to protect parents' rights. Ask for an application by contacting Home School Legal Defense Association, One Patrick Henry Circle, Purcellville, VA 20132, 540–338–5600, www.hslda.org.

■ ■ ■

Research Service

The National Home Education Research Institute (NHERI; listed in the Appendix) offers factual and documented information that will educate you about homeschooling. NHERI's materials are especially effective for informing skeptical grandparents and others such as friends, neighbors, and policymakers. Take a look at their Web site and catalog; the full-color booklet *Home Schooling on the Threshold: A Survey of Research at the Dawn of the New Millennium;* and the video *Home-Based Education: The Informed Choice.* These are particularly helpful for many purposes.

Special-Needs Children

The National Challenged Homeschoolers Associated Network (NATHHAN; listed in the Appendix) is a wonderful resource for those who may home educate children with special needs for example, those with learning disabilities or who are especially gifted or talented.[10]

Philosophy

Philosophy is a lofty-sounding word that often scares people. It refers to the love of wisdom and what is real, what is true, and what is of value. Your philosophy should guide your thinking and your actions. For example, I am a Christian. My philosophy is based on the truth that the Lord God has revealed Himself and truth to mankind by way of His general creation, His special revelation in the Bible, Jesus Christ's life on earth, and His Holy Spirit's guidance today.

You need to think about and decide what you believe. You need to base it on the truth of God's Word. Use His truth to guide all that you do in home education. Your philosophy, based on the Lord's truth, will guide you and help you to hold fast to what is true, real, and good. This philosophy will help you persevere, through good times and through times of adversity. It helps you to remember what is most important in life—your and your children's lives. You want to be sure that you are teaching your children the truth in all things.

Your philosophy should determine why you home educate your children. Your philosophy should guide your decisions about what to teach your children and how to do it. Your philosophy should guide you in deciding what books you read, what homeschool organization you support, in what local support group you participate, with whom your children associate, and, eventually, who (or what) your children will serve for a lifetime.

Conclusion

I have mentioned many topics and many things that you might do. This may seem a little overwhelming.

Perhaps it's time to stop, pray, and ask for God's guidance. It may also sound like this home education endeavor could cost a little money. Most good things do have a cost. Home education is worth it. The beginning of home education is often fraught with questions and worries. You may have wondered, *Is it legal? What will my parents (the children's grandparents) think? What about my child's teachers? What about socialization? How much will it cost? I only have a high school (secondary) education; how can I teach them algebra?* These are all common concerns, and thousands of parents have faced them—successfully.

Research and experience show that home education works. It works because it is consistent with God's plan for parents to have the primary role in the education and upbringing of their children. Home education also works because people like you have decided to homeschool, have relied upon God's help, and have given to their children the best they can possibly give them. May the Lord God bless you.

A PROFILE

Mary Pride

A mother of nine totally homeschooled children, Mary Pride first came to the attention of homeschool families in 1985 with the publication of *The Way Home*. This book pointed out the biblical and social reasons why mothers are needed at home. In that same year, her next project, *The Curriculum Buyer's Guide*, also appeared. This was the first book ever published that pulled together information on the dozen-and-a-half major packaged curricula then available to homeschoolers. The book reviewed each curriculum in depth and told homeschoolers how to obtain it. The next edition was renamed *The Big Book of Home Learning* and added reviews of hundreds of products organized by subject area. Since then, the various editions of *The Big Book of Home Learning* have continued to break new ground. For example, the latest edition (the fourth) includes reviews of online academies, many of which the Pride children have personally attended.

In 1993, Bill and Mary Pride founded *Practical Homeschooling* magazine, which has become known for its affable tone and cutting-edge research into new options for homeschoolers. The next year they founded the Homeschool World Web site, which is now the world's most-visited homeschool site. Through these means, they continue to encourage other homeschoolers to reach for and achieve greater levels of excellence.

Mary says: "I believe homeschooling will continue to grow as a movement, ultimately transforming into a movement for parent-led education, whether such education occurs in the home or elsewhere.

"The rise of homeschool co-ops, online academies, arrangements for ad hoc courses with private schools, and now the new University Model Schools, which combine homeschooling with complete parental control over how many courses children take in the school setting, are all ways homeschoolers are moving beyond the home, while still maintaining control over their children's curriculum and educational experiences.

"I'm hoping for a future where compulsory attendance laws are abolished, pre-K through 12 schools have the flexibility of a university crossed with a YMCA, and children and parents are free to pursue their educational dreams without state interference . . . just like I described 13 years ago in my book *Schoolproof.*

"I don't see secular homeschooling as ever outstripping Christian homeschooling, despite all the current media hoopla to the contrary, mainly because the Christian community and ethic is far more supportive of mothers at home. Big business might go through a phase of throwing big money at homeschool marketing, most of which will end up in the pockets of the so-called inclusive wing, but I believe the disappointing return on their marketing dollars will prevent any long-term distortion of the homeschool community by outside money. Government money, in the form of charter schools, could pose a greater threat to parental autonomy, but I hope the homeschool community will wise up to this quickly. As long as 'the hearts of the fathers are turned to the children,' God will be with us."

Contact: Practical Homeschooling, P. O. Box 1190, Fenton, MO 63026–1190, tel. 800–346–6322, Homeschool World, www.home-school.com.

■ ■ ■

Appendix

Homeschool Organizations Around the World

AUSTRALIA

The Australian Christian Academy
P. O. Box 5677 Brendale, QLD 4500
Australia
    tel. 61–07–3205–7444
    fax 61–07–3205–7331
    info@australianchristianacademy.org
    www.australianchristianacademy.org

Families Honouring Christ
P. O. Box 310
Mount Waverley VIC 3149
Australia
    tel. 03–9544–8792 or 03–9544–8792
    talldad@kepl.com.au

BRAZIL

Julio Severo
Rua José Sebastião Pereira Lima, 331
37958—000 Monte Santo de Minas, MG
Brazil
juliosevero@hotmail.com

BULGARIA

Ivaylo Tinchev
Bulgaria, Europe
Burgas, 8000
57 G. S. Rakovski Str., floor 5
  tel./fax +359 56 816 821
  homeschool@churchbg.com

CANADA

Contact the provincial-wide homeschool organization
for the province in or near where you live. Find a current listing of provincial organizations at:
The Teaching Home Web site
  www.teachinghome.com (click on "state and
  national organizations"

An excellent nationwide organization is:
Home School Legal Defence Association of Canada
(HSLDA)
2–3295 Dunmore Rd. SE
Medicine Hat, Alberta T1B 3R2
Canada
  tel. 403–528–2704
  fax 403–529–2694
  info@hsldacanada.org
  www.hsldacanada.org

CHILE

Kathleen McCurdy Burotto
  kathleen@familylearning.org

Czech Republic

Mical Semin, president
National Czech Home School Association
m.semin@volny.cz
semin@gts.cz

Germany

Schulunterricht zu Hause e.v. (School Instruction at Home)
registered seat: Buchwaldstrasse 16, 63303 Dreieich
Germany
   tel. 49–1805-SCHCUZH
   info@german-homeschool.de
   http://www.german-homeschool .de
   Contact person: Richard and Ingrid Guenther, Winterhaldenweg 48, 79856 Hinterzarten

Home Educators Are Real Teachers
PSC 3 Box 1581
APO 09021
Germany
   (011) 49–638–399–83–09 (from U.S.A.)
   wagnerwn@swol.de

Hungary

Karoly Gaspar Institute of Theology and Missions
Rev. Imre Scszokoe
3527 Miskolc, Kartacs u.1
Hungary
   tel. (011) 36–46–412–558
   kgtmi@axelero.hu

IRELAND

Homeschoolers of Ireland
c/o Elizabeth Bruton
Hillford House
Old Hill
Leixlip
Co. Kildare
    tel. (011) 353–16–244–567

JAPAN

CHEA of Japan
    Contact: Hiro Inaba
    HiroInaba@cheajapan.com
    www.cheajapan.com

HOSA
    Contact:Jun Adachi
    adachi8@email.msn.com
    www.homeschool.ne.jp

MEXICOLATINAMERICA

El Hogar Educador
APDO 17
Arteaga Coahuila 25350
Mexico
    tel. 52–0184830377
    vnm@characterlink.net
    www.elhogareducador.org
    Contact person: Mike Richardson
(U.S. address: 1001 S. 10th St. Ste.G PMB #529,
McAllen, TX 78501)

NETHERLANDS, THE

Nederlandse Vereniging voor Thuisonderwijs (Dutch
Association for Homeschoolers)
Postbus 761
1180 AT Amstelveen
  telefoonnummer (bericht inspreken) 084–8833044
  fax 084–8833044
  info@NVvTO.nl
  Mirah@dds.nl
  www.nvvto.nl

NEW ZEALAND

New Zealand Home Education Foundatioin
P.O. Box 9064
Palmerston North, New Zealand
  tel. 64637–4399
  hedf@xtra.co.nz
  www.homeeducationfoundation.org.nz

POLAND

Marek Budajczak, Ph.D.
Home School Organization
Stowarzyszenie Edukacji Domowej
ul.Drozdzynskiego 14
64–125 Ponicc; Polska - Poland
  tel. 0048/65/5731481
  homeed@poczta.onet.pl

PUERTO RICO/CARIBBEAN ISLANDS

Christian Home Educators of the Caribbean
Calle 10, E-19, Villa Universitaria
Humacao, PR 00791
  tel. 787–852–5672
  JCuret@compuserve.com

ROMANIA

Romanian Homeschool Association
Curcubet Gabriel
Str. Szentimre Nr. 55/A
Odorheiu Secuiesc
4150 Romania
tel. 402–662–10211
curcubetg@nextra.ro

SOUTH AFRICA

Pestalozzi Trust
Posbus 12332
Queenswood
0121 RSA
tel. 27–12–330–1337
fax 27–12–331–1018
defensor@pestalozzi.org
www.pestalozzi.org
Contact person: Leendert Van Oostrum

SWITZERLAND

Bildung zu Hause Schweiz
Swiss Homeschool Association
Postfach 868
8401 Winterthur
Switzerland
info@homeschool.ch
www.homeschool.ch
Contact person: Rudolf Schmidheiny

TAIWAN

Home Educators Fellowship
    lfpower@ms26.hinet.net
    skfan@tpts5.seed.net.tw
Karl Bunday
    kmbunday@ms29.hinet.net

UKRAINE

Andrew Okhotin
Russian Evangelistic Ministries
    okhotin@hotmail.com

UNITED KINGDOM/ENGLAND

The Home Service
48 Heaton Moor Road
Stockport
SK4 4NX
United Kingdom UK
    tel. 44–161–432–3782
    info@home-service.org
    www.home-service.org

UNITED STATES (AND TERRITORIES)

Contact the statewide homeschool organization for the state in which you live. Find a current listing of statewide organizations at:

The Teaching Home Web site
    www.teachinghome.com (click on "state and national organizations")

Two excellent nationwide organizations are:
National Home Education Research Institute (NHERI)
Home School Researcher (academic journal)
P. O. Box 13939
Salem, OR 97309–1939
    tel. 503–364–1490
    fax 503–364–2827
    mail@nheri.org
    www.nheri.org

Home School Legal Defense Association (HSLDA)
One Patrick Henry Circle
Purcellville, VA 20132
    tel. 540–338–5600
    fax 540–338–2733
    mailroom@hslda.org
    www.hslda.org

LAW

For current laws, contact the Home School Legal Defense Association (HSLDA) (listed in the Appendix under United States) or a similar organization in your nation.[1]

Endnotes

INTRODUCTION, THE HOMESCHOOLING REVOLUTION

1. Barbara Kantrowitz and Pat Wingert, "Learning at Home: Does It Pass the Test," *Newsweek*, June 12, 2000, 64–70. Retrieved 6/12/00 online http://newsweek.com/nw-srv/printed/us/sr/a20927–2000jun11.htm.
2. John Cloud and Julie Morse, "Seceding from School: Home Sweet School," *Time*, August 19, 2001, 46–54.
3. Mindy Sink, "Shootings Intensify Interest in Home Schooling," *New York Times*, August 11, 1999, A18.
4. Daniel Golden, "Home-Schooled Kids Defy Stereotypes, Ace SAT Test," *Wall Street Journal*, February 11, 2000, A1, A16.

CHAPTER 1, HOMESCHOOLING AT A GLANCE

1. Brian D. Ray, "Homeschooling in Canada," *Education Canada* 41, no. 1 (2001): 28–31; and, Patrick Basham, *Home Schooling: From the Extreme to the Mainstream* (Vancouver, BC, Canada: Fraser Institute, 2001. Retrieved 10/12/02 at http://www. fraserinstitute. ca/publications/pps/51/homeschool.pdf.
2. Lesley Ann Taylor and Amanda J. Petrie, "Home Education Regulations in Europe and Recent U.K. Research" *Peabody Journal of Education*: 75 (2000): 49–70.
3. Brian D. Ray, *Home Education Research Fact Sheet II* (Salem, OR: National Home Education Research Institute, 2001).

CHAPTER 2, NEW RESEARCH, NOW IN THE REAL WORLD: ADULTS WHO WERE HOME EDUCATED

1. Brian D. Ray, *Home Educated and Now Adults: Their Community and Civic Involvement, Views About Homeschooling, and Other Traits* (Salem, OR: National Home Education Research Institute, 2003). This major new study is available online www.nheri.org.
2. See Brian D. Ray, *Home Educated and Now Adults*, mentioned above, for more detail.

Chapter 3, The History, Growth, and Philosophy of Homeschooling

1. Thomas Alva Edison articles, http://www.minot. k12.nd.us/mps/edison/edison/edison.html; retrieved 12/2/00, http://www.thomasedison.com/biog.htm.
2. Edward E. Gordon and Elaine H. Gordon, *Centuries of Tutoring: A History of Alternative Education in America and Western Europe* (Lanham, MD: University Press of America, 1990).
3. James C. Carper, "Home Schooling, History, and Historians: The Past as Present," *The High School Journal*, April/May 1992, 254.
4. David B. Tyack, *The One Best System: A History of American Urban Education* (Cambridge, MA: Harvard University Press, 1974), 14–16.
5. Brian D. Ray, *Home Schooling on the Threshold: A Survey of Research at the Dawn of the New Millennium* (Salem, OR: National Home Education Research Institute Publications, 1999), 3.
6. J. Gary Knowles, Stacey E. Marlow, and James E. Muchmore, "From Pedagogy to Ideology: Origins and Phases of Home Education in the United States, 1970–1990," *American Journal of Education* 100 (1992): 204.
7. Michael Steven Shepherd, "The Home Schooling Movement: An Emerging Conflict in American Education" (Ed.D., dissertation, East Texas State University, 1986), 39–40; see also, Michael Steven Shepherd, "The Home Schooling Movement: An Emerging Conflict in American Education (an abstract)," *Home School Researcher*, September 1986, 1.
8. Knowles and others, "From Pedagogy to Ideology," 227.
9. Joseph Kirschner, "The Shifting Roles of Family and School as Educator: A Historical Perspective." In J. A. Van Galen and M. A. Pitman, eds., *Home Schooling: Political, Historical, and Pedagogical Perspectives* (Norwood, NJ: Ablex Publishing Corporation, 1991), 156.
10. J. Leo, "Sneer Not at 'Ozzie and Harriet,'" *U.S. News and World Report*, September 14, 1992, 24.
11. Maralee Mayberry, "Why Home Schooling? A Profile of Four Categories of Home Schoolers," *Home School Researcher* 4 (1988): 7–14.
12. Clint Bolick, (1987). "The Home Schooling Movement," *The Freeman: Ideas on Liberty* 37 (1987): 84.
13. For example, see the following titles by Brian D. Ray: *Home Schooling on the Threshold: A Survey of Research at the Dawn of the New Millennium* (Salem, OR: National

Home Education Research Institute Publications, 1999); *Home Education in New Mexico: Family Characteristics, Academic Achievement, and Social and Civic Activities* (Salem, OR: National Home Education Research Institute, 2001); *Home Education in Ohio: Family Characteristics, Academic Achievement, and Social and Civic Activities* (Salem, OR: National Home Education Research Institute, 2001). See also, Lawrence M. Rudner, "Scholastic Achievement and Demographic Characteristics of Home School Students in 1998," *Educational Policy Analysis Archives*, 7 (1999); retrieved 4/13/00 and earlier at http://epaa.asu.edu/epaa/ v7n8/; Maralee Mayberry, J. Gary Knowles, Brian D. Ray, and Stacey Marlow, *Home Schooling: Parents as Educators* (Newbury Park, CA: Corwin Press, 1995); Stacey Bielick, Kathryn Chandler, and Stephen Broughman, "Home Schooling in the United States: 1999" (NCES 2001–033) (Washington, DC: United States Department of Education); retrieved 8/2/00 at http://nces.ed.gov/pubsearch/pubsinfo.asp?pubid=200 033.

14. John Taylor Gatto, *The Underground History of American Education: A Schoolteacher's Intimate Investigation into the Problem of Modern Schooling* (Oxford, NY: Oxford Village Press, 2001), xxix.

15. For example, see Brian D. Ray, *Home Schooling on the Threshold: A Survey of Research at the Dawn of the New Millennium* (Salem, OR: National Home Education Research Institute Publications, 1999); Gayla C. Batterbee, "The Relationship of Parent-Child Interactive Systems to Cognitive Attributes in the Home Schooled Child" (Ph.D. dissertation, United States International University, 1992); Kurt J. Bauman, "Home Schooling in the United States: Trends and Characteristics) (working paper series no. 53; Washington, DC: U.S. Census Bureau, 2001); Stacey Bielick, Kathryn Chandler, and Stephen Broughman, *Home Schooling in the United States: 1999* (NCES 2001–033) (Washington, DC: United States Department of Education, 2001), retrieved online 8/2/01 at http://nces.ed.gov/pubsearch/pubsinfo.asp?pubid=2001033; Shirley Mae Breshears, "Characteristics of Home Schools and Home School Families in Idaho" (Ed.D. dissertation, University of Idaho, Moscow, 1996); Brian D. Ray, *Home Education in Ohio: Family Characteristics, Academic Achievement, and Social and Civic Activities* (Salem, OR: National Home Education Research Institute, 2001).

CHAPTER 4, BENEFITS TO CHILDREN AND YOUTH

1. Jon Wartes, *Five Years of Homeschool Testing Within Washington State* (Woodinville, WA: Washington Homeschool Research Project, 1991).
2. Brian D. Ray, "Homeschooling in Canada," *Education Canada* 41, no. 1 (2001): 28–31.
3. Mona Maarse Delahooke, "Home Educated Children's Social/Emotional Adjustment and Academic Achievement: A Comparative Study" (Ph.D. dissertation, California School of Professional Psychology, Los Angeles, 1986).
4. *Summary of SRA Testing for Centralized Correspondence Study April/May 1984* (Juneau, AK: Alaska Department of Education, 1985); *SRA Survey of Basic Skills and Alaska Statewide Assessment, Spring of 1985* [for Centralized Correspondence Study students] (Juneau, AK: Alaska Department of Education, 1986); *Results from 1981 CAT [for CCS]* (Juneau, AK: Alaska Department of Education, 1993); Bob Falle, *Centralized Correspondence School: Summary of the School District Report Card to the Public* (Juneau, AK: Alaska Department of Education, 1986); Bob Falle, "Standardized Tests for Home Study Students: Administration and Results," *Method: Alaskan Perspectives*, 7 (1986): 22–24.
5. Oregon Department of Education, Office of Student Services, *Annual Report of Home School Statistics, 1998–99;* Tennessee Department of Education, *Tennessee Statewide Averages, Home School Student Test Results, Stanford Achievement Test, Grades 2, 5, 7, and 9.*
6. Brian D. Ray, *Strengths of Their Own — Home Schoolers Across America: Academic Achievement, Family Characteristics, and Longitudinal Traits* (Salem, OR: National Home Education Research Institute, 1997).
7. Home School Legal Defense Association. (1994–1995). "Home Schoolers Score Significantly Above National Average," *Home School Court Report*, 10 No. 6, 3.
8. Lawrence M. Rudner, "Scholastic Achievement and Demographic Characteristics of Home School Students in 1998," *Educational Policy Analysis Archives*, 7 (1999). Retrieved 8/2/01 at http://epaa.asu.edu/epaa/v7n8/.
9. Brian D. Ray, *Home Education in Indiana: Family Characteristics, Reasons for Home Schooling, and Academic Achievement* (Salem, OR: National Home Education Research Institute, 1997).

10. Brian D. Ray, *Home Education in Massachusetts: Family Characteristics, Academic Achievement, and Social Activities* (Salem, OR: National Home Education Research Institute, 1998).

11. Brian D. Ray, *Home Education in Montana: Family Characteristics and Student Achievement* (Salem, OR: National Home Education Research Institute, 1990); Brian D. Ray, *Learning at Home in Montana: Student Achievement and Family Characteristics* (Salem, OR: National Home Education Research Institute, 1995).

12. Brian D. Ray, *Learning at Home in North Dakota: Family Attributes and Student Achievement* (Salem OR: National Home Education Research Institute, 1993).

13. Brian D. Ray, *Home Education in Oklahoma: Family Characteristics, Student Achievement, and Policy Matters* (Salem, OR: National Home Education Research Institute, 1992).

14. Howard B. Richman, William Girten, and Jay Snyder, "Academic Achievement and Its Relationship to Selected Variables Among Pennsylvania Homeschoolers," *Home School Researcher* 6 (1990): 9–16; Howard B. Richman, William Girten, and Jay Snyder, "Math: What Works Well at Home," *Home School Researcher,* 8 (1992): 9–19.

15. Paula Rothermel, "A Nationwide Study of Home Education: Early Indications and Wider Implications," *Education Now,* 24 (1999): 9.

16. Warren A. Nord, *Religion and American Education: Rethinking a National Dilemma* (Chapel Hill, NC: University of North Carolina Press, 1995), 160.

17. Steven W. Kelley, "Socialization of Home Schooled Children: A Self-Concept Study," *Home School Researcher,* 7 (1991): 9.

18. Richard G. Medlin, "Predictors of Academic Achievement in Home Educated Children: Aptitude, Self-Concept, and Pedagogical Practices," *Home School Researcher,* 10 (1994): 1–7.

19. Richard G. Medlin, "Home Schooling and the Question of Socialization," *Peabody Journal of Education* 75(2000): 107–23; Steven M. Kelley, "Socialization of Home Schooled Children: A Self-Concept Study," *Home School Researcher* 7 (1991): 1–12; Richard G. Medlin, "Predictors of Academic Achievement in Home Educated Children: Aptitude, Self-Concept, and Pedagogical Practices," *Home School Researcher* 10(1994): 1–7; John Wesley Taylor 5th, Self-Concept in Home-Schooling Children," *Home School Researcher* 2 (1986): 1–3.

20. Vicki D. Tillman, "Home Schoolers, Self-Esteem, and Socialization," *Home School Researcher*, 11 (1995): 5.

21. Mona Maarse Delahooke, "Home Educated Children's Social/Emotional Adjustment and Academic Achievement: A Comparative Study" (Ph.D. dissertation, California School of Professional Psychology, Los Angeles, 1986).

22. Norma S. Hedin, "Self-Concept of Baptist Children in Three Educational Settings," *Home School Researcher*, 7 (1991): 1–5.

23. Thomas C. Smedlay, "Socialization of Home School Children," *Home School Researcher*, 8 (1992): 12.

24. Larry E. Shyers, "A Comparison of Social Adjustment Between Home and Traditionally Schooled Students," *Home School Researcher*, 8 (1992): 1–8.

25. Brian D. Ray, *Strengths of Their Own—Home Schoolers Across America: Academic Achievement, Family Characteristics, and Longitudinal Traits* (Salem, OR: National Home Education Research Institute, 1997); Brian D. Ray, *Home Education in New Mexico: Family Characteristics, Academic achievement, and Social and Civic Activities* (Salem, OR: National Home Education Research Institute, 2001); Brian D. Ray, *Home Education in Ohio: Family Characteristics, Academic Achievement, and Social and Civic Activities* (Salem, OR: National Home Education Research Institute, 2001).

26. Steven D. Smith, Jilanne Bannink-Misiewicz, and Shelly Bareman, "A Comparison of the Fundamental Motor Skill Abilities of Home School and Conventional School Children," *Home School Researcher* 8 (1992): 1–8.

27. Sonia K. Gustafson, "A Study of Home Schooling: Parental Motivation and Goals," *Home School Researcher*, 4(1988): 2, 4–12.

28. Steven F. Duvall, D. Lawrence Ward, Joseph C. Delquadri, Charles R. Greenwood, "An Exploratory Study of Home School Instructional Environments and Their Effects on the Basic Skills of Students with Learning Disabilities," *Education and Treatment of Children*, 20 (1997): 150–72.

29. Steven F. Duvall, D. Lawrence Ward, Joseph C. Delquadri, Charles R. Greenwood, "An Exploratory Study of Home School Instructional Environments and Their Effects on the Basic Skills of Students with Learning Disabilities," *Education and Treatment of Children*, 20 (1997): 66.

30. Katheryn Kearney, *At Home in Maine: Gifted Children and Homeschooling.* G/C/T, (1984): 6.

31. Jacque Ensign, "Defying the Stereotypes of Special Education: Homeschool Students" (paper presented to the annual meeting of the American Educational Research Association, San Diego, CA, April 1998).

32. Ibid., 6–7.

33. Christopher J. Klicka, *Home Schooling: The Right Choice* (Nashville; Broadman & Holman, 2000).

34. Linda R. Montgomery, "The Effect of Home Schooling on the Leadership Skills of Home Schooled Students," *Home School Researcher,* 5(1989: 1–10.

35. Susannah Sheffer, *A Sense of Self: Listening to Homeschooled Adolescent Girls* (Portsmouth, NH: Boynton/Cook Publishers, Heinemann, 1995), 2, 122–23, 176.

36. Rhonda A. Galloway, "Home Schooled Adults: Are They Ready for College?" (paper presented at the annual meeting of the American Educational Research Association, San Francisco, CA, April 1995, San Francisco CA), 18.

37. *ACT High School Profile; Home Schooled Composite Report; HS Graduating Class 1997* (Iowa City, IA: American College Testing, 1997).

38. Geoff Barber of Educational Testing Service to Brian D. Ray, February 20, 2001, personal communication on SAT summary reporting.

39. Paulo C. M. de Oliveira, Timothy G. Watson, and Joe P. Sutton, "Differences in Critical Thinking Skills Among Students Educated in Public Schools, Christian Schools, and Home Schools," *Home School Researcher,* 10 (1994): 1–8.

40. Rhonda A. Galloway and Joe P. Sutton, "College Success of Students from Three High School Settings: Christian School, Home School, and Public School" (paper presented at the annual meeting of the National Christian Home Educators Leadership Conference, Boston, MA, October 1997.

41. Irene M. Prue, "A Nationwide Survey of Admissions Personnel's Knowledge, Attitudes, and Experiences with Home Schooled Applicants" (Ph.D. dissertation, University of Georgia, Athens, 1997), 62.

42. Christopher J. Klicka, *Home School Students Excel in College: Special Report* (Purcellville, VA: Home School Legal Defense Association, 1998), 3.

43. Christine Foster, "In a Class by Themselves," *Stanford Magazine,* November/December 2000. Retrieved 12/4/00 online http://www.stanfordalumni.org/jg/mig/

news_magazine/magazine/novdec00/articles/home-schooling.html.

44. J. Gary Knowles and K. de Olivares, "Now We Are Adults: Attitudes, Beliefs, and Status of Adults Who Were Home-educated as Children" (paper presented at the annual meeting of the American Educational Research Association, Chicago, IL, April 1991); J. Gary Knowles and James A. Muchmore, "Yep? We're Grown-Up Home Schooled Kids—And We're Doing Just Fine, Thank You Very Much" *Journal of Research on Christian Education* 4 (1995): 35–56.

45. Brian D. Ray, *Home Education in New Mexico: Family Characteristics, Academic Achievement, and Social and Civic Activities* (Salem, OR: National Home Education Research Institute, 2001).

46. Patricia M. Lines, "Homeschooling: Private Choices and Public Obligations," *Home School Researcher* 10 (1994): 21.

47. Charles S. Clark, "Home Schooling: Is It a Healthy Alternative to Public Education?" *The CQ* [Congressional Quarterly] *Researcher,* 4 (1994): 769–92.

48. Christian Smith and David Sikkink, "Is Private Schooling Privatizing?" *First Things* 92 (1999): 16–20.

49. Brian D. Ray, *Strengths of Their Own—Home Schoolers Across America: Academic Achievement, Family Characteristics, and Longitudinal Traits* (Salem, OR: National Home Education Research Institute, 1997). This major new study is available online at www.nheri.org/

50. Gregory J. Marchant, "Home Schoolers On-line," *Home School Researcher* 9 (1993); 8.

51. Brian D. Ray, *Strengths of Their Own—Home Schoolers Across America: Academic Achievement, Family Characteristics, and Longitudinal Traits* (Salem, OR: National Home Education Research Institute, 1997).

52. Brian D. Ray, *Home Education in New Mexico: Family Characteristics, Academic Achievement, and Social and Civic Activities* (Salem, OR: National Home Education Research Institute, 2001).

53. Esther Shein, "Teaching at Home? Your PC Can Make a Difference (Web PCs—For School and Play)," *Gateway Guide,* 2001, 16–19.

54. Jennie F. Rakestraw, "Home Schooling in Alabama," *Home School Researcher,* 4 (1988): 1–6; Joan Ellen Havens, "A Study of Parent Education Levels as They Relate to Academic Achievement Among Home Schooled Children" (Ed.D. dissertation., Southwestern

Baptist Theological Seminary, Fort Worth, TX, 1991); Brian D. Ray, *A Nationwide Study of Home Education: Family Characteristics, Legal Matters, and Student Achievement* (Salem, OR: National Home Education Research Institute, 1990); Brian D. Ray, *Home Education in Oklahoma: Family Characteristics, Student Achievement, and Policy Matters* (Salem, OR: National Home Education Research Institute, 1992); Brian D. Ray, *Strengths of Their Own—Home Schoolers Across America: Academic Achievement, Family Characteristics, and Longitudinal Traits* (Salem, OR: National Home Education Research Institute, 1997); Brian D. Ray, Homeschooling in Canada," *Education Canada* 41 (2001): 28–31.

55. Steven F. Duvall, D. Lawrence Ward, Joseph C. Delquadri, Charles R. Greenwood, "An Exploratory Study of Home School Instructional Environments and Their Effects on the Basic Skills of Students with Learning Disabilities" *Education and Treatment of Children,* 20 (1997): 150–72; Steven F. Duvall to Brian D. Ray, January 23, 1999, personal communication.

56. Brian D. Ray, *Learning at Home in Montana: Student Achievement and Family Characteristics* (Salem, OR: National Home Education Research Institute, 1995).

57. Richard G. Medlin, "Predictors of Academic Achievement in Home Educated Children: Aptitude, Self-Concept, and Pedagogical Practices. *Home School Researcher* 10 (1994): 1–7.

58. Jennie F. Rakestraw, "Home Schooling in Alabama," *Home School Researcher,* 4 (1988): 1–6; Joan Ellen Havens, "A Study of Parent Education Levels as They Relate to Academic Achievement Among Home Schooled Children" (Ed.D. dissertation., Southwestern Baptist Theological Seminary, Fort Worth, TX, 1991); Brian D. Ray, *Home Education in Oklahoma: Family Characteristics, Student Achievement, and Policy Matters* (Salem, OR: National Home Education Research Institute, 1992); Brian D. Ray, *Strengths of Their Own—Home Schoolers Across America: Academic Achievement, Family Characteristics, and Longitudinal Traits* (Salem, OR: National Home Education Research Institute, 1997).

59. Brian D. Ray, *A Nationwide Study of Home Education: Family Characteristics, Legal Matters, and Student Achievement* (Salem, OR: National Home Education Research Institute, 1990); Brian D. Ray, *Home Education*

in North Dakota: Family Characteristics and Student Achievement (Salem, OR: National Home Education Research Institute, 1999); Jon Wartes, *The Relationship of Selected Input Variables to Academic Achievement Among Washington's Homeschoolers* (Woodinville, WA: Washington Homeschool Research Project, 1990); Lawrence M. Rudner, "Scholastic Achievement and Demographic Characteristics of Home School Students in 1998," *Educational Policy Analysis Archives*, 7 (1999); retrieved 2 August 2001 online http://epaa.asu.edu/epaa/v7n8/.

60. Jon Wartes, *The Relationship of Selected Input Variables to Academic Achievement Among Washington's Homeschoolers* (Woodinville, WA: Washington Homeschool Research Project, 1990), 50; see also, J. S. Coleman, E. Campbell, C. Hobson, J. McPartland, A. Mood, F. Weinfeld, and R. York, *Equality of Educational Opportunity* (Washington, DC: U.S. Office of Education, National Center for Educational Statistics, 1966); James S. Coleman and Thomas Hoffer, *Public and Private High Schools: The Impact of Communities* (New York: Basic Books, 1987), chapter 5; Catherine E. Snow, Wendy S. Barnes, Jean Chandler, Irene F. Goodman, and Lowry Hemphill, *Unfulfilled Expectations: Home and School Influences on Literacy* (Cambridge, MA: Harvard University Press, 1991).

61. Brian D. Ray, *Home Education in North Dakota: Family Characteristics and Student Achievement* (Salem, OR: National Home Education Research Institute, 1999); Brian D. Ray, *Home Education in Oklahoma: Family Characteristics, Student Achievement, and Policy Matters* (Salem, OR: National Home Education Research Institute, 1992); Brian D. Ray, *Strengths of Their Own— Home Schoolers Across America: Academic Achievement, Family Characteristics, and Longitudinal Traits* (Salem, OR: National Home Education Research Institute, 1997); Terry Russell, "Cross-validation of a Multivariate Path Analysis of Predictors of Home School Student Academic Achievement," *Home School Researcher* 10 (1994): 1–13; Brian D. Ray, *Home Education in New Mexico: Family Characteristics, Academic Achievement, and Social and Civic Activities* (Salem, OR: National Home Education Research Institute, 2001).

62. Brian D. Ray, *A Nationwide Study of Home Education: Family Characteristics, Legal Matters, and Student Achievement* (Salem, OR: National Home Education Research Institute, 1990); Jon Wartes, *The Relationship*

of Selected Input Variables to Academic Achievement Among Washington's Homeschoolers (Woodinville, WA: Washington Homeschool Research Project, 1990); Lawrence M. Rudner, "Scholastic Achievement and Demographic Characteristics of Home School Students in 1998," *Educational Policy Analysis Archives*, 7 (1999); retrieved 8/2/01 at http://epaa.asu.edu/epaa/v7n8/.

63. Brian D. Ray, *A Nationwide Study*; Brian D. Ray, *Strengths of Their Own — Home Schoolers across America: Academic Achievement, Family Characteristics, and Longitudinal Traits* (Salem, OR: National Home Education Research Institute, 1997).

64. Brian D. Ray, *A Nationwide Study of Home Education: Family Characteristics, Legal Matters, and Student Achievement* (Salem, OR: National Home Education Research Institute, 1990); Brian D. Ray, *Strengths of Their Own — Home Schoolers across America: Academic Achievement, Family Characteristics, and Longitudinal Traits* (Salem, OR: National Home Education Research Institute, 1997); Brian D. Ray, *Home Education in New Mexico: Family Characteristics, Academic Achievement, and Social and Civic Activities* (Salem, OR: National Home Education Research Institute, 2001); Lawrence M. Rudner, "Scholastic Achievement and Demographic Characteristics of Home School Students in 1998," *Educational Policy Analysis Archives*, 7 (1999); retrieved 8/2/01 online http://epaa.asu.edu/epaa/v7n8/.

65. Tracy Romm, "Home Schooling and the Transmission of Civic Culture" (Ed.D. dissertation, Clark Atlanta University, Atlanta, GA, 1993), 307, 351.

66. Daniel Smithwick to Brian D. Ray, December 5, 2001, personal communication; April 10, 1998. Smithwick is executive director of the Nehemiah Institute.

CHAPTER 5, HOW HOMESCHOOLING AFFECTS THE FAMILY AND PARENTS

1. Jon Wartes, *Effects of Homeschooling upon the Education of the Parents: Comments from the Field* (Woodinville, WA: Washington Homeschool Research Project, 1992), 25.

2. World Congress of Families II convened November 14–17, 1999, in Geneva Switzerland, where about 1,600 delegates and participants representing 275 pro-family organizations from 65 nations took part; retrieved the purpose of the World Congress of Families online 8/6/01 at http://www.worldcongress.org/WCF/wcf_purpose.htm

3. Maralee Mayberry, J. Gary Knowles, Brian D. Ray, and Stacey Marlow, *Home Schooling: Parents as Educators* (Newbury Park, CA: Corwin Press, 1995), 45.
4. Shirley Mae Breshears, "Characteristics of Home Schools and Home School Families in Idaho" (Ed.D. dissertation, University of Idaho, Moscow. 1996), 74.
5. Suzanne Harrison, "A Qualitative Study of Motivational Factors for Choosing to Homeschool: Experiences, Thoughts, and Feelings of Parents" (Ph.D. dissertation, Gonzaga University, Spokane WA, 1996).
6. Jon Wartes, *The Relationship of Selected Input Variables to Academic Achievement Among Washington's Homeschoolers* (Woodinville, WA: Washington Homeschool Research Project, 1990), 25.
7. Allan Carlson, "Preserving the Family for the New Millennium: A Policy Agenda," *The Family in America*, 9 (1995): 7.
8. Jayn Allie-Carson, "Structure and Interaction Patterns of Home School Families," *Home School Researcher* 6 (1990): 11–18.
9. Ronald E. Page, "Families Growing Together: A Study of the Effects of Home Schooling on the Development of the Family" (master's thesis, Maryvale Institute, Birmingham, England, 1997), 5.
10. Shirley Mae Breshears, "Characteristics of Home Schools and Home School Families in Idaho" (Ed.D. dissertation, University of Idaho, Moscow, 1996); Elizabeth Baurle Treat, "Home School Literacy: An Ethnographic Study of Parents Teaching Reading and Writing" (Ph.D. dissertation, University of Pennsylvania, 1990; Elizabeth Baurle Treat, "Parents Teaching Reading and Writing at Home: An Ethnographic Study," *Home School Researcher*, 6 (1990): 9–19; Jon Wartes, *Effects of Homeschooling upon the Education of the Parents: Comments from the Field* (Woodinville, WA: Washington Homeschool Research Project, 1992).
11. Wartes, *Effects of Homeschooling upon the Education of the Parents,"* pages 50, 46, 46, 62, and 57, respectively.
12. Shirley Mae Breshears, "Characteristics of Home Schools and Home School Families in Idaho" (Ed.D. dissertation, University of Idaho, Moscow. 1996); Bernice Marie Mahan and Brenda Joyce Ware, *Home-Schooling: Reasons Some Parents Choose This Alternative Form of Education, and a Study of the Attitudes of Home-Schooling Parents and Public School Superintendents Toward the Benefits of Home-Schooling*

(Washington, D.C.: ERIC Document Reproduction Service No. ED286624, 1997); Maralee Mayberry, J. Gary Knowles, Brian D. Ray, and Stacey Marlow, *Home Schooling: Parents as Educators* (Newbury Park, CA: Corwin Press, 1995); Brian D. Ray, *Home Education in Indiana: Family Characteristics, Reasons for Home Schooling, and Academic Achievement* (Salem, OR: National Home Education Research Institute, 1997); Tracy Romm, "Home Schooling and the Transmission of Civic Culture" (Ed.D. dissertation, Clark Atlanta University, Atlanta, GA, 1993); Susannah Sheffer, *A Sense of Self: Listening to Homeschooled Adolescent Girls* (Portsmouth, NH: Boynton/Cook Publishers, Heinemann, 1995), 137; Stacey Bielick, Kathryn Chandler, and Stephen Broughman, *Home Schooling in the United States: 1999* (NCES 2001–033) (Washington, DC: United States Department of Education); Kurt J. Bauman, "Home Schooling in the United States: Trends and Characteristics" (working paper series no. 53; Washington, DC: U.S. Census Bureau, 2001).

13. Allan Carlson, "Will the Separation of School and State Strengthen Families? Some Evidence from Fertility Patterns," *Home School Researcher*, 12 (1996): 2.

14. Kay C. James, "Transforming America," *Imprimis* 25(1996): 1.

15. Jon Wartes, *Effects of Homeschooling upon the Education of the Parents: Comments from the Field* (Woodinville, WA: Washington Homeschool Research Project, 1992), 35.

16. Ibid.

17. Eric Buehrer, *The Public Orphanage: How Public Schools Are Making Parents Irrelevant* (Dallas, TX: Word Publishing, 1995).

18. Daniel Golden, "Home-Schooled Kids Defy Stereotypes, Ace SAT Test," *Wall Street Journal*, February 11, 2000, A1.

19. Jon Wartes, *Effects of Homeschooling upon the Education of the Parents: Comments from the Field* (Woodinville, WA: Washington Homeschool Research Project, 1992), 34.

20. Patricia M. Lines, "Homeschooling: Private Choices and Public Obligations, *Home School Researcher* 3 (1994): 21.

21. *New Research* is published by the Howard Center, 934 North Main Street, Rockford IL 61103, (815) 964–5819, www.profam.org; see also, Shankar Vedantam, "Kid Care, Behavior Linked in Study: Aggression, Defiance Seen Across the Board," *Washington Post*, April 19, 2001.

22. Matthew 6:21 NKJV.

23. Malachi 4:4–6 NKJV.
24. Shannon Brownlee and Matthew Miller, "Lies Parents Tell Themselves About Why They Work," *U.S. News and World Report*, May 12, 1997, 58–64; Arlie Russell Hochschild, *The Time Bind: When Work Becomes Home and Home Becomes Work* (New York: Henry Holt and Company, 1997).

CHAPTER 6, HOW HOMESCHOOLING AFFECTS SOCIETY

1. Sandy Chapin and Harry Chapin, "Cats in the Cradle," [Story Songs, Ltd., ASCAP], on record album *Harry Chapin's Greatest Stories—Live* (Los Angeles, CA: Electra Records), 1976.
2. "National Survey Commissioned by the National Center for Fathering: Fathers Involvement in Their Children's Learning" (Shawnee, KS: National Center for Fathering, 1999); table; retrieved 12/6/01 http://www.fathers. com/research/involvement.html.
3. Shannon Brownlee and Matthew Miller, "Lies Parents Tell Themselves About Why They Work," *U.S. News and World Report*, May 12, 1997, 58–64.
4. *New Research* is published monthly as an accompaniment to *Family in America*, and both are published by The Howard Center, 934 North Main Street, Rockford IL 61103, www.profam.org.
5. Jon Wartes, *Effects of Homeschooling upon the Education of the Parents: Comments from the Field* (Woodinville, WA: Washington Homeschool Research Project, 1992), 25.
6. Ibid., 17.
7. Brian D. Ray, *Strengths of Their Own—Home Schoolers Across America: Academic Achievement, Family Characteristics, and Longitudinal Traits* (Salem, OR: National Home Education Research Institute, 1997).
8. Allan C. Carlson, *From Cottage to Work Station: The Family's Search for Social Harmony in the Industrial Age* (San Francisco, CA: Ignatius Press, 1993), 168.
9. Weldon M. Hardenbrook, *Missing from Action: Vanishing Manhood in America* (Nashville, TN: Thomas Nelson Publishers, 1987), 55.
10. Allan Carlson, "Will the Separation of School and State Strengthen Families? Some Evidence from Fertility Patterns," *Home School Researcher*, 12 (1996): 1–5.
11. John Barratt Peacock, "The Why and How of Australian Home Education" (Ph.D. dissertation, LaTrobe University, Bundoora, Victoria, Australia, 1997).

12. Rockne McCarthy, Donald Oppewal, Walfred Peterson, and Gordon Spykman, *Society, State, and Schools: A Case for Structural and Confessional Pluralism* (Grand Rapids, MI: William B. Eerdmans Publishing Co., 1991), 85.

13. Ibid.

14. As cited in Sheldon Richman, *Separating School and State: How to Liberate America's Families* (Fairfax, VA: Future of Freedom Foundation, 1994), 51.

15. Wartes, *Effects of Homeschooling upon the Education of the Parents*, 34.

16. Ibid.

17. Michael W. Apple, "The Cultural Politics of Home Schooling," *Peabody Journal of Education* 75 (2000): 256–71.

18. Christopher Lubienski, "Whither the Common Good? A Critique of Home Schooling," *Peabody Journal of Education*, 75 (2000): 207–32.

19. Patricia M. Lines, "Homeschooling: Private Choices and Public Obligations, *Home School Researcher* 3 (1994): 16.

20. Brian D. Ray, "Home Schooling for Individuals' Gain and Society's Common Good," *Peabody Journal of Education* 75, no. 1 and 2 (2000): 272–93.

21. Ibid., 287, 288.

Chapter 7, I'm a Teenager and I Want to Homeschool

1. Proverbs 24:3–6 NIV.

2. Exodus 20:12 NIV.

3. To obtain copies of the author's 24-page, full-color booklet *Home Schooling on the Threshold: A Survey of Research at the Dawn of the New Millennium*, contact the National Home Education Research Institute, www.nheri.org, also listed in the Appendix.

4. Christopher J. Klicka, *Home Schooling: The Right Choice* (Nashville; Broadman & Holman, 2000).

5. David Callihan and Laurie Callihan, *The Guidance Manual for the Christian Home School: A Parent's Guide for Preparing Home School Students for College or Career* (Franklin Lakes, NJ: Career Press), 2000.

6. Theodore E. Wade Jr. and others, *The Home School Manual: Plans, Pointers, Reasons, and Resources*, 7th ed. (Berrien Springs MI: Gazelle Publications, 1998).

7. Ingle P. Cannon, *Mentoring Your Teens* (Taylors, SC: Education Plus, 1999).

8. Grace K. Llewellyn, *The Teenage Liberation Handbook: How to Quit School and Get a Real Life and Education* (Eugene, OR: Lowry House Publishers, 1998).

9. Susannah Sheffer, *A Sense of Self: Listening to Homeschooled Adolescent Girls* (Portsmouth, NH: Boynton/Cook Publishers, Heinemann, 1995).

10. John Taylor Gatto, *The Underground History of American Education: A Schoolteacher's Intimate Investigation into the Problem of Modern Schooling* (Oxford, NY: Oxford Village Press), 2000/2001.

11. Ibid., xxv.

12. Sheldon Richman, *Separating School and State: How to Liberate America's Families* (Fairfax, VA: Future of Freedom Foundation, 1994).

13. Charles L. Glenn, *The Myth of the Common School* (Amherst, MA: University of Massachusetts, 1988).

CHAPTER 8, WHICH APPROACH TO HOMESCHOOLING?

1. This chapter is based in many ways on an article this author wrote and published in conjunction with the United States Department of Education: Brian D. Ray, *Homeschooling Teaching Strategies* [ERIC Digest #EDO-SP-2000–6, 2 pp.] (Washington, DC: United States Department of Education, ERIC Clearinghouse on Teaching and Teacher Education, 2000). Retrieved 3/6/01 online http://www.ericsp.org/pages/digests/home_schooling.html. References related to the statements and summaries in this chapter are furnished in the ERIC Digest.

2. Peter A. Cohen, James A. Kulik, and Chen-Lin Kulik, "Educational Outcomes of Tutoring: A Meta-analysis of Findings," *American Educational Research Journal* 19 (1982): 237–48; Jennifer Fager, *Tutoring: Strategies for Successful Learning* (Washington, D.C.: ERIC Reproduction Service No. ED431840, 1996).

3. Michael Pearl and Debi Pearl, *To Train Up a Child* (Pleasantville, TN: 1994).

4. J. Richard Fugate, *What the Bible Says about Child Training*, 2d ed. (Elkton, MD: Full Quart Press), 1998.

5. Susan A. McDowell, and Brian D. Ray, eds., "The Home Education Movement in Context, Practice, and Theory," special issue of *Peabody Journal of Education*, 75 (2000).

6. This author is also indebted to the work of *The Teaching Home* magazine (Box 20219, Portland OR 97294, tel. (503) 253–9633, http://www.teachinghome.com/) related to the topic of educational approaches and methods

one may use in homeschooling. Please see their Web site at www.teachinghome.com and especially the section and articles on "getting started" (for example, 29 November 2001 online http://www.teachinghome.com/started/index.cfm).

7. Patrick Farenga of Holt Associates to Brian D Ray concerning definition of *unschooling*, June 15, 2000, personal communication. See also information at http://www.holtgws.com.

8. Samuel L. Blumenfeld, *How to Tutor,* 2d ed. (Boise, ID: Paradigm Co., 1986).

9. Brian D. Ray, *Strengths of Their Own—Home Schoolers Across America: Academic Achievement, Family Characteristics, and Longitudinal Traits* (Salem, OR: National Home Education Research Institute, 1997); Brian D. Ray, "Home Schooling: The Ameliorator of Negative Influences on Learning?" *Peabody Journal of Education,* 75 (2000): 71–106.

10. Alan Thomas, *Educating Children at Home* (London and New York: Cassell, 1998), 127.

CHAPTER 9, ODDS AND ENDS—MORE COMMON QUESTIONS

1. Terry Dorian and Zan Tyler, *Anyone Can Homeschool: How to Find What Works for You* (Lafayette, LA: Huntington House Publishers, 1996).

2. Brian D. Ray, *Strengths of Their Own—Home Schoolers across America: Academic Achievement, Family Characteristics, and Longitudinal Traits* (Salem, OR: National Home Education Research Institute, 1997).

3. Brian D. Ray, *Home Education in New Mexico: Family Characteristics, Academic Achievement, and Social and Civic Activities* (Salem, OR: National Home Education Research Institute, 2001).

4. Brian D. Ray, *Ensuring Scientific Literacy* (audiotape). (Salem, OR: National Home Education Research Institute, 2001.

CHAPTER 10, LEARNING MORE OR GETTING STARTED IN HOMESCHOOLING

1. Christopher J. Klicka, *Home Schooling: The Right Choice* (Nashville: Broadman & Holman, 2000).

2. Gregg Harris, *The Christian Home School* (Gresham, OR: Noble Publishing Associates, 1995).

3. Brian D. Ray, *Home Schooling on the Threshold: A Survey of Research at the Dawn of the New Millennium* (Salem, OR: National Home Education Research Institute Publications, 1999).

4. Michael Pearl and Debi Pearl, *To Train Up a Child* (Pleasantville, TN: 1994); J. Richard Fugate, *What the Bible Says about Child Training*, 2d ed. (Elkton, MD: Full Quart Press of Holly Hall Publications), 1998.

5. Michael P. Farris, *The Home Schooling Father* (Nashville: Broadman & Holman, 1999).

6. Home School Legal Defense Association, One Patrick Henry Circle, Purcellville VA 20132, (540) 338–5600, www.hslda.org.

7. Homeschooling USA, PO Box 3338, Idaho Springs CO 80452, (303) 457–4092, www.homeschoolingusa.com.

8. Home Run Enterprises, 16172 Huxley Circle, Westminster CA 92683.

9. Home Life, PO Box 1190, Fenton MO 63026, www.home-school.com.

10. National Challenged Homeschoolers Associated Network, PO Box 39, Porthill ID 83853, (208) 267–6246, nathanews@aol.com, www.natthan.com.

APPENDIX

1. An excellent way to get very current listings for many homeschool organizations is to go to the Teaching Home Web site at: www.teachinghome.com (click on "state and national organizations," and then "foreign" for other than North America).

Index